The Mobility Revolution

Lukas Neckermann

The Mobility Revolution

Zero Emissions
Zero Accidents
Zero Ownership

Matador
9 Priory Business Park
Kibworth Beauchamp
Leicestershire LE8 0RX, UK
Tel: (+44) 116 279 2299
Fax: (+44) 116 279 2277
Email: books@troubador.co.uk
Web: www.troubador.co.uk/matador

ISBN 978 1784622 473

Cover design by Nils Poschwatta.
Visit: www.nilsposchwatta.de
Edited by Richard Lane

For more information, please visit
www.threezeroes.com

British Library Cataloguing in Publication Data.
A catalogue record for this book is available from the British Library.

Typeset in Garamond and Avenir by Troubador Publishing Ltd
Printed and bound in the UK by TJ International, Padstow, Cornwall

Matador is an imprint of Troubador Publishing Ltd

Disclaimer

Contents

Chapter 5:
Outlook and Impact of the Three Zeroes 135

Introduction

I thoroughly enjoy driving. Few things fill me with the same sense of bliss and freedom as piloting a roadster along a twisting mountain road on a sunny day. In reality, however, this type of driving has become infrequent for city-dwellers like me. It is not without regret that I admit this is likely a good thing.

As a consultant and entrepreneur with a sizable carbon footprint, clearly my credentials and interests in this area are more capitalist than environmental. Nevertheless, old-school transportation progressively fills me with doubt and guilt. It is inefficient, destructive of our planet and a disservice to generations to come. Having lost a loved one to an automobile accident, my tolerance of the avoidable fatality rate on the world's roads has also evaporated. I know that I am not alone in this, but part of a mind-shift that's sparking a new revolution in mobility.

We are on the cusp of a transformation very much akin to the Industrial and Internet revolutions. This book will outline the three key forces of this new revolution. Naturally, it's futile to make concrete predictions on where, when and to what extent changes will take place, but I assure you they will happen sooner than we think. I will begin to paint a picture of our world after the Three Zeroes have taken effect. Just as the Internet altered far more than merely how we communicate, the impacts of the Mobility Revolution will be felt more widely than in solely the automobile industry.

The benefits of the Mobility Revolution will be on par with finding a cure for AIDS, with more than one million lives saved each year from prevented vehicle accidents. It goes beyond this, however. Seven million lives are lost each year because of pollution, which suggests that, given current urbanization trends, the Three Zeroes will eventually lead to billions of lives improved by reductions in emissions and improvements in air quality.

Economically speaking, the waste from underutilized vehicle assets, infrastructure, city spaces and time is in the trillions, regardless of currency. This development will also begin to be addressed by the Three Zeroes.

The book you're holding isn't meant to be a comprehensive, technical dissection of the automotive world. Instead, it is intended to provoke discussion, guide decisions and perhaps encourage investment in our new future of mobility. After reading it, I hope you'll agree that the Mobility Revolution can't come soon enough.

Lukas Neckermann, November 2014

Chapter 1:

The Future Of Mobility

" There is considerable logic in eliminating humans from the driving equation. **"**

Thirty years ago we watched a fictional Michael Knight call his self-driving Pontiac Trans Am sports car, KITT, via his wristwatch. KITT then drove the heroic agent autonomously to his destination.

While the storyline (and acting) in *Knight Rider* remains dubious – and the Pontiac brand meanwhile is history – Hollywood's technological vision of the future today no longer appears absurd. It is not a leap of faith and imagination any more for us to have speech recognition in our wristwatches, cars that navigate themselves and dialogue between vehicles on the street – technologies that will in due course give us the choice of being driven by our cars. Spending fruitless, frustrated hours behind the wheel, dodging other cars, cursing at bad drivers, getting lost and polluting the environment will be going the way of Pontiac in just a few years.

If we believe that technology exists to make our lives easier and to increase efficiency, then the future of mobility is about removing three key sources of inefficiency and nuisance from the driving equation. That means doing away with combustion engines, human operation and vehicle ownership.

The Three Zeroes

To outline why we stand at the cusp of the Mobility Revolution, let me first provide an overview of where the road is taking us and briefly explain the concept of Three Zeroes, before delving into greater detail in the coming chapters. (The final chapter of the book will focus on the impacts of the Mobility Revolution on the automobile industry and other sectors of our economy.)

Zero emissions. Most of us have become familiar with the sociopolitical and environmental factors that are leading toward a carbon-conscious society. Global warming is at an alarmingly high level and consequently there are pressures from consumers and governments to slash vehicle emissions.

Big industry, and particularly the auto industry, is being blamed for the emissions that poison our planet, destroy the atmosphere and trigger natural disasters with apparently increasing frequency. Putting aside a discussion on the magnitude of impact from vehicles, and disregarding a handful of mistaken global-warming cynics in the US, the common consensus is that human behaviour – especially in relation to our transportation needs – is at the source of our environmental ills.

Governments (both state and national), international non-governmental organizations, manufacturers and the public at large have more or less bought into the desire to reduce emissions, albeit with varying levels of commitment and differing tools. But whatever the target or whichever incentive or penalty is used, the automobile industry stands before a major transformation. In contrast to the oil crisis of the 1970s or the late '90s electric vehicle mini-boom in California, today the aspiration and motivation to improve vehicle efficiency is being matched with the ability and necessity to amend urban and transport infrastructure (energy storage and wired and wireless charging) in parallel. This change lies at the heart of this book's message.

Zero accidents. Today, according to the World Health Organisation, more than 1.2 million people die in road traffic accidents worldwide annually, making it a top ten global killer, between heart disease and acquired immunodeficiency syndrome, or AIDS. Staggeringly, over ninety percent of these deaths are due to some kind of human error, and are therefore avoidable. Imagine twenty full narrow-body aircraft disappearing every single day. We certainly wouldn't accept this in air travel; we cannot accept it on our roads, either. In the same way that technology has in fact reduced air travel deaths to close to zero by introducing automation into the cockpit, so too will autonomous vehicles reduce road fatalities to almost nothing.

There is considerable logic in eliminating humans from the driving equation. Given an alternative, what incentive is there to take a mode of transport that puts you at a significantly increased risk of death? For us to close in on zero accidents it's not enough to build bigger, quicker, more plentiful airbags, or tougher safety cells in cars. We need to reduce the key source of collisions: human error. The vehicle should be guided by something devoid of distraction and emotion.

While self-driving vehicles are still at the fringes of consciousness for most, the truth is that many autonomous driving features are already found in mass-market vehicles today. Thanks to the advent of GPS navigation systems our cars have a better idea of where they are going than we do. By relying on ubiquitous parking-assist cameras and alarms we have already started to accept that sensors can see more than the driver in the immediate vicinity of the vehicle.

Google's self-driving car has driven well over one million law-abiding miles around California and Nevada without self-induced incident. As a result, governments in more than thirty US states are working to implement laws legalizing autonomous driving. Governments the world over (including the UK,

Germany, Sweden and Japan) are scrambling to follow suit. No politician worth his or her salt would want to stand in the way of significant reductions in automobile accidents.

Beyond cars we've seen self-driving vehicles in many forms, such as subway trains, various monorails and in mining applications. These systems without drivers have both greater efficiency and lower accident rates. They are also more punctual and save on costs. Autonomous drones, farm tractors and parking transport systems (such as the ones at London Heathrow airport and Disneyworld) already paint a picture of robot-drivers as 'normal'.

Naturally, the proliferation of autonomous transport relies upon a raft of changes and raises numerous questions, some of which we'll address in later chapters. If driving no longer has to be regulated, for instance, can traffic enforcement resources be put to better use? If we don't need to park close to our destination, what will happen to city streets and parking infrastructure (which today takes up a surprisingly high proportion of urban space)? What is the effect on public transportation and on taxis? Will autonomous vehicles expedite or inhibit urbanization? How will the fifteen million people living in the US who are visually or physically impaired, and who would gain greater mobility using such technology, be better integrated into the workplace? What will happen to automotive retail as car-sharing replaces purchasing outright and electric vehicles poison the well of constant business from servicing and oil changes? How will insurance companies react? (*The Insurance Journal* rightly speculated in 2012, *Will Driving Become Too Safe to Insure?* Without accidents many insurers as they exist today are toast. They are reliant on both the revenues and cash flows of mandatory car-insurance premiums, which are calculated on the basis of accident rates.)

Construction, real estate, logistics and freight forwarding, infrastructure maintenance and public transportation are just some of the industries that are also impacted as we move toward vehicle automation.

How Ownership is Passé!

Last but not least is zero ownership. The combination of urbanization, resource reprioritization, the availability of delivery services (for just about anything and at any time) and the dawn of autonomous mobility means that personal ownership of cars is gradually becoming pointless.

A baby born this year will likely no longer get a 'driving' licence at sixteen or eighteen years of age, the way we have done for over one hundred years. They won't need to as they won't own a car, and neither will their friends. They will find it makes no sense to bind capital in an asset that stays idle for twenty-one or twenty-two of twenty-four hours in a day. Car ownership is already making less sense to many people, especially in urban areas, as research shows. A 2014 Deloitte study titled *The Changing Nature of Mobility* noted a significant decrease in the intention to own a vehicle among Generation Y (aka Millennial) respondents, especially in urbanized countries such as Japan. This was matched with a growing preference for alternate modes of transportation in all countries studied. In the same way that Airbnb is providing an alternative to second home ownership (a home that would only rarely be used), car-sharing is providing a sensible option as a second car for many. As the trend becomes ubiquitous it will also begin to replace the 'first' car. Therefore, I suggest that within the Mobility Revolution the number of cars owned outright will be greatly reduced, while we as consumers are enabled and motivated to purchase *mobility* itself.

Here again, eager politicians join economic and social trends. As with the electrification and autonomy of vehicles, governments are taking initiatives to promote car-sharing as a solution for clogged city streets. Primitive car-sharing has existed for decades, with carpooling widely encouraged throughout Western countries. The Dutch government even formed a foundation for shared car use over 20 years ago: 'Stichting voor Gedeeld Autogebruik'. The institution was based on the idea and philosophy that you don't need to own a car in order to drive one, and was the first of many national, independent organizations for mobility providers, carrying out research and promoting the concept of car-sharing. The main focus on forming this and many similar associations was on supporting and 'educating' people about the key roles and benefits of car-sharing clubs.

Nudge Theory Toward the Three Zeroes

'Nudge theory' is a term widely used in scientific fields such as behavioural science and economics. It was popularized by Richard Thaler's 2008 book Nudge: Improving Decisions about Health, Wealth, and Happiness. The premise behind the theory is based on a belief that in order to get people to carry out certain actions they should be given appropriate positive reinforcement as well as indirect suggestions. This motivates people through incentives to carry out a certain action without the use of force.

This book will also address governmental roles in moving toward the Three Zeroes. Using political, economic, social or legal force to alter the behaviour of society is simply unnecessary and inefficient, whereas employing a combination of incentives and disincentives in achieving a greater good gently moves society toward a desired goal. As I will discuss in later chapters, governments are using approaches based on nudge theory to support vehicle electrification and eliminate barriers to achieving autonomy.

What the Future Will Look Like As We Head Toward the Three Zeroes

In cities worldwide, smartphone apps can now help you find a shared ride, car-service or an available taxi nearby within minutes. Uber, Hailo, GetTaxi, Lyft, BlaBlaCar, as well as Sidecar and Ridejoy promote the use of on-demand mobility and ride-sharing. These options currently still complement public transport and taxis, although in some cities there are now more Uber drivers than taxi drivers. More importantly, they are a transitional step toward fully autonomous fleets of electric personal transit vehicles designed expressly for this new purpose.

The series of pictures in our head would a decade ago have seemed like a scene from a sci-fi movie, but today it becomes clear, attainable and realistic. In fact, it's not entirely dissimilar to the *Knight Rider* example I mentioned earlier. Simply add that the vehicles will

- not be proprietary (i.e. you or Knight Industries won't own it)
- no longer be powered by typical internal-combustion engines
- not need to be refilled or refueled incessantly (as this will occur wirelessly via inductive charging built into dedicated lanes, as on the cover of this book)
- be very quiet

So, what does the big picture look like? An integrated transport system that merges on-demand, autonomous, emissions-free, personal and public transport for short and long distances into a seamless network that will link cities and individuals to one other, picking people up and delivering them to their destinations. Guided by a link to our calendars and address books, mobility management software will suggest when we have to leave, at what time we'll arrive and how we'll get there. Based on our personal preferences, the network can recommend the optimal combination of personal, shared and public transport, proactively avoiding hindrances, accidents, the need for parking and stress.

This coordinated, interlinked network of automated electric buses, cars, trucks and motorcycles will reduce the risk of accidents to nearly zero for drivers, passengers and pedestrians. Charged by renewable energy sources, it will eliminate emissions from cities and revert personal car ownership and driving back to something that is desired, rather than required. In the same way some of us still appreciate vinyl records instead of MP3s on occasion, or, more pertinently, the way horse riding is still practised for enjoyment rather than primary transportation in developed countries, we may still want to drive around that snaking mountain road in an electric, non-autonomous convertible. But for everyday use we will rely on the mobility network, just as we today blindly rely on iTunes and Spotify to select our day-to-day music, rather than take the LP out of its sleeve.

Our city and extra-urban infrastructure will gradually adapt to this model, with facilities for charging, parking (or not parking), renting and using a variety of new mobility solutions beyond the 'two-mode' model of personal transport we've come to know.

Our infrastructure – that is, the homes we live in, the streets we use, the offices we will work in (assuming we will work in offices) and the online web we weave – will also adapt to this new paradigm, which will

- eliminate the useless (inner-city parking lots, gas stations and taxi-circling) and
- facilitate the efficient (wireless charging lanes, drop-off and pick-up points and autonomous vehicle-update zones).

Our lives will more seamlessly move between mobile and stationary modes – whether we are on the road, at home or at a place of work, we will be online and aware, able to work, learn, communicate, inform, purchase or share, and innovate without interruption – if we so choose.

This is what the future of mobility in our world will be like.

Bicycles in the Mobility Revolution

Strangely, the bicycle still seems unfashionable as a third mode of transport in most cities. Uber (who we will discuss in greater detail in later chapters) and its clones provide a 'third mode' of transportation for city-dwellers – between walking and taking one's own car. These companies aim to cover distances usually undertaken by taxis. Statistically, Uber users in San Francisco, for example, are actually travelling distances that are, at a pinch, walkable, but definitely bikeable.

In a survey of 1,000 Americans in Boston, Chicago, New York, Austin, San Francisco and Washington DC (conducted by SASAKI), fifty-eight percent said that cars remain their primary mode of transportation, twenty-nine percent use public transportation, ten percent walk, and only two percent use bicycles. Clearly, outside of the City of Portland, the US has quite a distance to go until bicycles are even considered relevant.

Nevertheless, efforts abound in making bicycles easy, available and accessible. Last-mile bike-renting offers such as Citibikes in New York, Boris Bikes in London, and Vélib' in Paris exist in over 500 cities worldwide (making up a fleet of over one million bicycles worldwide, supported by city councils eager to remove cars from the streets). In order to popularize this third mode of transportation even more, infrastructure is key. After Copenhagen and Amsterdam's well-established bike infrastructure, London's aims might be the most ambitious. It has developed a proposal for a £220-million cross-city 'Skycycle bicycle superhighway', with the aim of increasing cycling commutes by 400 percent by 2025 (compared to 2000 levels). The UK further supports bicycle ownership with considerable tax benefits.

A sizable hitch is that bicycles are erroneously seen as a dangerous alternative transportation option and therefore disregarded as part of a solution for more sustainable mobility. This, in spite of the fact that seven times more people lose their lives as pedestrians and twenty times more because of automobile accidents than on bicycles in the US each year. The media doesn't help. Every bicycle accident seems to make the news in city newspapers, while car accidents are accepted as a part of everyday life and go unreported. Anecdotally, most of us know someone who has lost a loved one in a car accident – few know someone who has died in a bicycle collision.

Perhaps in a world of autonomous shared electric vehicles, the perceived danger of riding bicycles will subside. But until this happens they will continue to have a place as a parallel mode of transportation, dividing society into bike users and non-bike users. Their development will mirror that of automobiles: they will rapidly become electrified (or hybridized, with pedal-power for flats and electric motors for hills, charging the batteries again during the descents); they will add navigation capacity and safety technologies; and (electric or semi-electric) bicycle-sharing will continue to expand in cities where the infrastructure allows it.

There are two key global drivers (among the many social benefits) that will spur evolution during the mobility revolution: commercial motivations and demographic shifts.

Commercial Incentives

Time usually spent driving around the city or stuck in traffic has traditionally been seen as a sunk cost – an unavoidable expense in the effort to pursue economic rent.

Today, alternatives exist so that this time can be used to increase social interaction with one another or take care of more effective tasks. From a social standpoint this might support community and families, which is desirable. Even more interesting, however, is the economic viewpoint; autonomy will significantly improve our productivity, which is what makes this an attractive proposition to governments and industry.

It is also a great way to improve marketing endeavours. As Google earns all of its profits from advertising, it's no secret that the intent behind the Google car is to allow riders to spend their time watching advertisements or introducing them to great new products that they can then order or buy while aboard (and we should expect the Apple car, or perhaps even an Amazon Fire car to achieve this same goal). The possibilities are endless, limited only by one's imagination to make use of a network that is as efficient as mobility can get.

Changing Demographics

Key statistics on urbanization

More than seventy-five percent of Europeans and North Americans already live in urban areas. The *global* proportion of city-dwellers has surpassed half of the world's population (fifty-three percent in 2013, according to the World Bank) and is expected to top seventy percent by 2050, making urbanization the most significant and fastest lifestyle shift in the history of humankind.

Some figures:

- The world's current urban population is 3.5 billion, yet by the year 2030 this number is estimated to rise to five billion. Peeking into the future, by 2100 the world's urban population will be somewhere between 6.4 and 8.4 billion – in other words, more people will be living in urban areas than the entire *current* population of Earth.
- In 1800, the only city in the world with a population greater than one million was Beijing. By 1900, fifteen more cities had been added to this list, and a century later the count had increased to a staggering 378 cities. That number is estimated to almost double to 600 cities by the end of 2025.
- New York City was the first urban area in the world to have a population of ten million, in 1950. In 1962, Tokyo became the first incorporated city with a population of ten million. To date, *just a half-century later*, twenty-one additional cities have been added to this list. Within the next decade seven more megacities are projected to emerge, all but one (Kinshasa) within Asia.
- China is reported to have the greatest rate of urban expansion. On an annual basis growth varies from 13.3 percent in coastal regions to 3.9 percent in western areas. According to McKinsey, China builds five cities the size of Chicago every two years and will have more than 220 such cities within the next decade.
- Including the wider metropolitan area, Tokyo-Yokohama is considered to be the largest urban area in the world with a population of 36.7 million spread over 13,500 square kilometres. It alone constitutes two percent of global GDP.
- Urban areas cover one percent of the world, yet account for three-quarters of total energy requirements while emitting eighty percent of greenhouse gases.

As we approach a stage where around three-quarters of the world's population will live in urban areas, quality of life becomes a social and political imperative. But why do we love to live and congregate in cities? Gary Lawrence, Chief Sustainability Officer at Aecom, noted at the Business for Social Responsibility Conference in 2012: "I don't think cities exist to aggregate interesting architecture and infrastructure. Cities exist because there is some sort of compact between citizen and community that their life has a better chance of getting better by choosing to live in an urban place."

The notion of cities offering a better quality of life for individuals, and being key to the development of society, has been explored in significant detail by noted urbanist Richard Florida, author of *The Rise of the Creative Class,* Professor at New York University as well as Director at the University of Toronto's Rotman School. He argues that cities themselves create the fertilized soil for thought and development: "They have long been the vehicles for mobilizing, concentrating, and channeling human creative energy."

As such, we shouldn't vilify cities. Research in the US and EU suggests that people *want* to live in urban areas (ideally walkable ones). *Fast Company Magazine* in August 2014 cited a survey indicating that architecture, food, public parks and proximity to, well, everything are key reasons to live and enjoy cities. *Monocle Magazine* makes an annual spectacle of its world's top twenty-five 'liveable' cities survey, chronicling architecture, public transportation, tolerance and culture among the key features that make – in 2014 – Copenhagen, Tokyo, Melbourne and Stockholm the top four in the world (*Monocle* itself is based in London, which ironically doesn't make it into the top 10, but I'm assured by editor Tyler Brûlè would be top 30).

Urbanization is not the real problem here, then. Cities are efficient and effective in their use of space, resources and infrastructure. People generally live in smaller dwellings and travel shorter distances than they do in rural areas. It's the concentration of people and transportation in a limited space, however, which poses problems in terms of emissions and quality of life.

How, then, do planners ensure that their cities accomplish the lofty mission of unleashing creative and transformative development unto the world? Jeff Speck, author of *Walkable City, How Downtown can save America, One Step at a Time,* notes that 'wealth, health, and sustainability' are three key elements in the development of cities. He rightly insists that walkability is key to the further development of cities, but also concedes that a combination of various modes of transport is infinitely preferable to the automobile as a single homogenous mode.

So, if urbanization holds within it the key to our future, city governments and urban planners must heed the statistics and trends, and enable technologies that will allow for the continued growth of cities without further increases of pollution concentration and traffic gridlock.

This book focuses on the changing outlook for mobility, the effects of which will bring tremendous tumult to one of the biggest industries in the world. As mentioned, however, ripples will be much more widely felt in all associated industries as well as in the way we live, work, consume and socialize.

It's our duty to find and implement initiatives that deal with global threats and promote growth at the same time, thereby improving the quality of our city-dweller lives while promoting the overall trajectory of our planet's wellbeing. For urban development, this means that we must build in a way that reduces energy use as well as total emissions at a macro level.

In order to change the landscape of automotive specifically, it's crucial that any alternate and renewable energy sources or technologies developed are cost efficient as well. These technologies can help save the climate and solve the energy crisis. Traffic jams that result in millions of tons of needless emissions each year, for instance, can be diminished by a gradual but persistent focus on the Three Zeroes.

Modern, efficient transport systems require less energy and so reduce total daily emissions from vehicles; choosing trains rather than personal automobiles for a trip leads to a thirty percent or more reduction in energy consumption. Opting for efficiency within public transport takes it a step further – the hybrid buses in Sao Paulo and London, for example, emit twenty to thirty percent less carbon dioxide than their traditional counterparts. Fully-electric buses, such as the ones used in San Francisco, much of Eastern Europe and many cities in China have the potential to take this yet again a step further (currently these are connected to wires, like trams, but battery technology presents an opportunity for these networks to become as wireless as your telephone). The city of Gumi, South Korea, was the first with an incipient network of electric buses that charge wirelessly on the move. Paired with renewable energy, the network represents the ultimate expression of zero-emissions public transport in the world today.

These transport systems are not only energy-efficient, they also reduce inner-city emissions while cutting commuting time. An efficient transport system will mean that people spend less time stuck in traffic behind the wheel of their car with more time to carry out higher-priority tasks.

How Wise is buying a Car After all?

CNN asked in 2008: "Is America's suburban dream collapsing into a nightmare?" Is it still a dream to own a house and a car in American suburbs? Is it really wise to spend a substantial amount of money in order to own a car and become part of an unpleasant and inefficient system? Who wants to spend two hours in traffic every day? Taking into account the price of fuel and social cost of emissions, is there any satisfaction or even benefit left in owning a car and do we end up paying more in terms of time and money, relatively speaking, than we spent on a car? What is the point of ownership if the output is just a fraction of all that goes into owning a car? *Time Magazine* concluded in April 2014: "The new American dream is living in a city, not owning a house in the suburbs."

The tide is shifting toward New Urbanism (according to CNN), where:

- "Rundown downtowns are being revitalized by well-educated, young professionals who have no desire to live in a detached single-family home typical of suburbia where life is often centred around long commutes and cars."
- "Unlike their parents, who calculated their worth in terms of square feet, ultimately inventing the McMansion (vastly oversized houses that have crept up in suburban neighbourhoods, termed after the fast-food chain), this generation is more interested in the amenities of the city itself: great public spaces, walkability, diverse people and activities with which they can participate," said Ellen Dunham-Jones, a professor of architecture and urban design at Georgia Tech.

For the automotive industry this means that people will stop – fairly suddenly, when presented with options – spending money buying vehicles that require them to be stuck in traffic congestion for hours on end in order to get home.

Urbanization, Efficiency and Licensing

The idea – held by some – that urbanization is a cause of pollution, as well as social and environmental ills, is nothing but a myth. It is a proven fact that cities are more efficient in providing work and amenities for citizens, requiring less space and energy for living and thereby leading to a better overall ecological balance. People live in considerably smaller abodes; heat generated in one apartment is not lost through the walls to the countryside, but is absorbed and transferred to neighbouring flats. City-dwellers travel shorter distances and have more options for transport in cities than rural areas (that is not to say, however, that the time spent on transport is necessarily less).

As urbanization accelerates, the number of transport options, be they public, shared or even the aforementioned bicycle, increases. So perhaps it's not surprising to see that the trend (at least in developed economies in Europe and North America) is matched by a decrease in young people acquiring driving licences. Simply put – why bother, when I have a ton of alternatives? While eighty-seven percent of citizens of driving age living in rural areas of the UK hold a driving licence, only sixty-two percent of Londoners do, according to Daniel Newman at Cardiff University. Mike Munger of Duke University concludes: "City living takes the shine off the car."

Not only are younger drivers no longer getting driving licences, they correspondingly are opting for fewer, or even not owning vehicles, as well.

Globally the impact is even greater and is being realized more quickly. In the same way that entire generations of people on the Indian subcontinent and in Africa have leapfrogged interim technologies, never having known landline telephones (adopting mobile phones as their first digital communication tools), there will eventually be a generation of middle-class, post-millennials, who will grow up entirely without a licence.

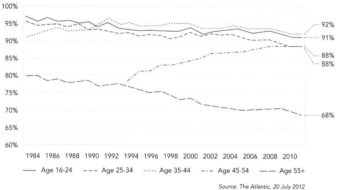

Licensed Drivers by Age Group (U.S.)

Source: The Atlantic, 20 July 2012

In western economies, new generations diverge from their parents, for whom a car was a sign of achievement and success; they see cars as a hindrance to their own advancement in a connected economy. With a considerable sample of over 11,000 respondents in forty-six US cities, the 2014 Mobility Attitudes Study by the Transit Center (housed at the University of Wisconsin) is one of the more comprehensive studies on what

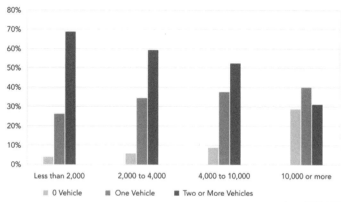

Percent of Households by Vehicle Ownership and Population Density (US 2009)

Source: NHTS, 2009

I'll call the 'post-ownership' generation. It summarized: "The Millennial generation seems to be defying its sheltered, suburban upbringing by delaying the acquisition of a driver's licence and choosing transit... As the cohort ages and has children, at least some are surely considering whether they will ever return to the car-centric lifestyle of their youth. It is incumbent upon policy makers, transit agencies, and citizen groups to seize the moment by accommodating and capitalizing on these attitudes and bringing those maturing millennials (and many slightly older adults) into a car-free middle age."

While today drivers still fret about finding parking spaces or the next filling station, in another decade or two owning an internal-combustion car will be like smoking cigarettes – something that was done in a bygone age, or by an older generation who can't quit.

Isn't There a Better Solution?

An inefficient transport system, such as individual car ownership and single-person vehicle journeys, only increases the problems of modern life. People who continue to live far from their workplace face issues every day that could be easily be reduced or negated entirely.

The potential for an impending traffic crisis brought on by mass urbanization is actually an opportunity to make life better for citizens. In order to improve the state of transport systems and align them with a city's environmental strategies, a momentous and highly necessary push will come from governments, involving political, social and financial incentives. By initiating laws and imposing fees and restrictions (bridge-tolls, combustion-charging zones and low-emission zones) as well as fines, people will be not-so-gently encouraged to refrain from using their car and adopt car-sharing initiatives, as well as shift to electric cars.

By similarly urging (nudging, pushing, forcing) manufacturers to introduce fuel-efficient and environmentally-friendly vehicle options, governments can shift the trend from petroleum-based vehicles to emissions-free transport, be it battery-electric or hydrogen-storage-electric (thereby also reducing a reliance on foreign oil). Yet those with political influence also need to ensure that transportation is cost-efficient – they need to ensure electric vehicles are affordable in order to reach a critical mass of adoption. Improvements will also be made in public transport systems so that people are encouraged to combine use of personal transport with public transport networks. Solutions are already being devised and funded that will motivate people to make a shift toward efficient, multi-modal approaches to their transport requirements.

Generation Y and Generation Z (generally known as the *Digital Natives* globally or the *post 9/11 generation* in the US) especially recognize that there are superior solutions to most of their needs, and are consequently no longer willing to tie up huge amounts of capital in assets that they will use only sparingly.

A new sensibility about ownership and usage has sparked the sharing economy (and the third part of this book, Zero Ownership). A great example for this is Airbnb, formed when the founders successfully offered travellers 'bed and breakfast' on an air mattress in their living room. The company now offers almost one million different places available to rent from individuals in the most popular destinations around the world. For some this eliminates the need to purchase vacation homes, as people have access to 'homes' away from home for as long as they want, ranging from boats to apartments to castles, all dependent on their budgets and desires. For others, it has eliminated the need for hotel rooms when staying in another city.

Lastly, we have come to accept the computing powers inherent in smartphone applications, which will allow for seamless combinations of options for current locations and destinations that riders can select. Our telephones have the connectivity and computing power to plan out routes in real-time, command vehicles and fares, and allow you to pay for everything without cash.

We will experience a world where our mobility will be controlled through apps that will manage all vehicles necessary for transportation, including ferries, buses, cars and bikes, creating a system that is smooth and coordinated.

Seamless Mobility – a Finnish Model?

An on-demand sharing-economy project is in progress in the Finnish capital Helsinki, where a plan to transform the public transport system is due for completion in 2025. The city wants to create a public-transport network based entirely around 'mobility on demand', eliminating the need to own cars and revolutionizing traditional scheduled public transportation. This system would allow people to plan transport and purchase rides directly via their smartphones – combining the benefits of ride-sharing (Uber etc.) with the cost-efficiency of public transport. The idea is to provide a wide and flexible variety of riding options available to the general public at a rate so attractive that people are driven away from private ownership of cars. The network will major in expediency and simplicity, with the consequence that people would naturally prefer the new mobility system rather than owning a car.

Of course, the planning and implementation of this mobility network is easier in a city like Helsinki, as almost every citizen owns a smartphone and the relatively homogenous social structure means that most can afford the fares for the rides (which are slightly higher than an average bus ride but cheaper than a taxi ride). The relative wealth and high technology adoption rates have made it easier for the government to design a public transport system that can be used by everyone in the city. However, the question still arises: will this same system work for any other city (think of Mumbai, Mexico City, or Bucharest), keeping in mind the purchasing power of every citizen in the country as well as necessary smartphone penetration rates?

Isabel Dedring, Deputy Mayor of London for Transport, noted in an interview for this book: "Key goals for any urban transport network are to make it as accessible, safe, reliable and efficient as possible. In London there are twenty-seven million trips a day, often on networks that are reaching capacity – for example, the Tube will start to approach running forty trains per hour in the coming decade. We see advances in technology as a way for us to continue to deliver increases to efficiency and reliability, both within a mode and through multi-modal integration. These changes will happen in part naturally due to the evolution of social media and related tools; the interesting question for cities is what role they will be best suited to play in facilitating this process."

Chapter 2:

Zero Emissions

" What is needed to save our world for our grandchildren is not simply technological evolution but a transformative shift. **"**

Air Pollution is Killing Us

For years we've taken the future of our planet for granted, continuing with habits that gradually destroy our environment, making us our own worst enemies. Even now, when air, water and soil pollution has reached catastrophic levels in many places, and global warming has led to again, in 2014, the warmest year on public record, some countries in the world maintain a short-term approach, ignoring the long-term sustainability of our planet and future generations of humans.

According to estimates released by the World Health Organization (WHO), in 2012 an estimated *seven million people* lost their lives as a consequence of air pollution. That puts air pollution at the top of the list of health risks caused by environmental factors on a global scale. Therefore, our discussion is not about reducing air pollution because it *might* kill people; millions of lives *are* indisputably lost due to this single cause. If serious actions are not taken this trend will continue, increasing in intensity.

Beyond the obvious culprit, carbon dioxide, particulate

emissions are leading to unspeakable death rates. WHO notes: "Mortality in cities with high levels of particulates exceeds that observed in relatively cleaner cities by fifteen percent to twenty percent." The air is so poisonous in some cities that it is unsafe for inhalation. WHO has declared particulates in the air a 'group one' carcinogen – on a par with Asbestos – that leads to heart attacks and lung cancer. Roughly 1,600 cities have dangerously high levels of airborne particulate matter, out of which the highest levels were found in India. New Delhi has the global highest airborne particulate matter content in its air – forty percent of residents suffer from some kind of respiratory ailment. At a level of 153 micrograms, New Delhi's average levels are fifteen times the threshold that is considered safe according to WHO standards. Similarly high levels have been observed in cities in Pakistan and Bangladesh, but the problem is by no means reserved for countries of the Indian subcontinent. London's airborne particulate matter is the highest in Europe, and greater than Beijing's in certain locales. *BusinessWeek* reported on a Public Health England (a government agency) finding in June 2014: "In addition to NO_2, diesel combustion also generates easily inhaled fine particulate matter, which probably killed 3,389 people in London in 2010." Marylebone Road and Regent Street – popular tourist destinations – were the worst offenders. Stuttgart – home to Daimler and Porsche – has the dubious honour of coming second in Europe, with particulate matter concentrations also twice the level permitted by the EU.

Airborne particulate matter, or PM2.5, is so-called because of the diameter in microns of particles including ammonia, sulfate, carbon and various nitrates. These particles are tiny enough that they easily enter the bloodstream, causing cancer and other deadly diseases.

In 2014 China for the first time began emitting more

carbon dioxide per capita than the EU. With a population over 1.2 billion that means China's total carbon dioxide emissions represent twenty-eight percent of the world's total – higher than the EU and the US combined – and are on an utterly unsustainable upward trajectory. While Chinese cities are not yet on the list of cities with the highest particulate matter, their severe carbon dioxide emissions mean residents suffer from air pollution of a different kind. Due in large part to the fact that over 80% of the country's energy needs are being met by coal-fired power plants, China's cities are filled with a grey smog that prompts urbanites to travel behind masks at all times to protect themselves from its harmful effects. The country's leaders have (at least publicly) declared a war against pollution; in November 2014 China's President Xi Jinping agreed with US President Barack Obama to raise the proportion of China's zero-carbon energy-generation to twenty percent by *around* 2030. Environmentalists note this to be wholly insufficient, as in the interim China continues to build two new coal-fired power plants *per week*.

While it may be tempting for western governments to shift blame and ask China to 'clean up its act', it's important to remember the emissions that are created also come from factories producing goods going to the West. The real blame thus lies with unbridled consumption and unmanaged transportation.

A Message From Above

The Synthesis Report from the United Nations Intergovernmental Panel on Climate Change (IPCC) comes to an indisputable conclusion: "Human influence on the climate system is clear and growing, with impacts observed on all continents. If left unchecked, climate change will increase the likelihood of severe, pervasive and

Global Carbon Dioxide Levels Double,
Breaking out of 800,000 Year Trend.
Global Temperature Levels Clearly Linked and Rising.

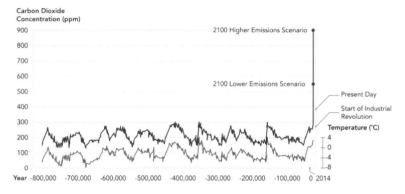

irreversible impacts for people and ecosystems." The chart above – generated from IPCC data – illustrates patently that global temperature levels and carbon dioxide levels have been correlated for over 800,000 years. Since the Industrial Revolution (in other words – in the last 200 or so years) we have broken out of this 800,000-year cycle, with carbon dioxide levels currently over 400 ppm, and projected to double once again by 2100 – leading to a best-case increase in average temperatures of plus two degrees Celsius, and a worst-case increase of plus eight degrees. While this doesn't sound like much, this effectively means a global climatic catastrophe that on the one hand will exacerbate the severity of droughts in places like the southwestern US and southern Asia, and on the other hand – due to polar icecaps melting and the expansion of water masses – will flood most low-lying cities (including New York, Guangzhou, Mumbai, and Miami). As Laurence Smith notes in his impressive book The New North: The World in 2050, "the total exposed population is forecast to grow more than threefold, to 150 million people" worldwide by 2070, and, "The economic exposure is forecast to rise more than tenfold... to nine percent of global GDP."

To my mind, the facts are scientifically and objectively clear. Carbon dioxide and particulate emissions are already killing us today, and causing dramatic global warming that will inhibit future life on our planet. Yet there remain a few, insular, self-serving and unyielding doubters who, against all evidence, either contest that climatic change is make-believe or think that we are not contributing to it.

'Insular' as they represent a minute proportion of capitalists and scientists, and 'self-serving' because their denial is generally about preserving the status quo of their own businesses. Rather than supporting a common cause for preserving the planet, their defiance (and debunking their misguided conspiracy theories) costs governments in the US and EU billions.

At least in the US, there seems to be some correlation between deniers of global warming and rejecters of evolution. Perhaps they require a message from above, beyond the dramatic increase in tsunamis, hurricanes and flooding in highly populated areas? Well before the famed, 192-page encyclical in 2015, where he effectively blamed human selfishness for global warming, Pope Francis himself had already pronounced climate change to be "Our sin, exploiting the Earth and not allowing her to give us what she has within her." In a statement, the Pope said: "Human action which is not respectful of nature becomes a boomerang for human beings that creates inequality," and propagates what Pope Francis has termed "the globalization of indifference."

Similarly, Archbishop Desmond Tutu in September 2014 declared climate change a "deep injustice" where

*"deadly storms, heat waves, droughts, rising food prices –
are being visited on the world's poor." He called an
international boycott of mining, oil and other companies
involved in the trade of fossil fuels.*

*Perhaps the world of 2020, 2050, or 2070 seems a
bit too far away for the deniers. However, if a few million
Christians are moved to believe climate change and boycott
oil companies, the economic case to steer against
environmental destruction will become clearer.*

The Contribution of Cars

Transportation is the source of thirty percent of all emissions
responsible for global warming, according to the Pew Center on
Global Climate Change. The global warming that is leading to
climate change is endangering our food supplies, water supplies,
our health and our homes as well as putting our national security
at risk. Record high temperatures, floods caused by melting
icebergs and glaciers as well as forest fires and merging seasons are
some of the signs that the Earth is getting warmer. Of transport-
system-generated emissions, the majority come from cars and
trucks, meaning road-based vehicles are responsible – very roughly
speaking – for almost one-fifth of the world's air pollution.

Each gallon of gas consumed results in a hefty twenty-four
pounds of total emissions. Of that, five pounds come from the
extraction process of petroleum as well as the production and
delivery processes. The remaining nineteen or so pounds of
emissions come in the form of energy release (to overcome
friction, be it rolling resistance or aerodynamic drag). These
add up to a staggering total released into the atmosphere per
car. On average, every car emits roughly six tons of emissions
annually, consisting chiefly of carbon monoxide.

All else being equal, the obvious aim should be either to eliminate tailpipe emissions by switching to electric vehicles or choosing vehicles that emit considerably less greenhouse gases per pound of fuel burnt. While tightening governmental emissions rules and forcing a shift to greater fuel efficiency (effectively just 'a little less death than before') is a nice temporary solution, emissions are nevertheless still adding up to aggravate the environment. Greater fuel efficiency may slow down the effects of harmful emissions but it will not solve the problem. What is needed to save our world for our grandchildren is not simply technological evolution but a transformative shift – much like the Industrial Revolution.

Energy Dependence and the Governmental Imperative to Support Innovation

Interestingly, around the time of the Industrial Revolution, innovation in mobile energy generation and storage was at a peak and automobile manufacturers came up with ideas that used various sources of energy instead of only the method popular today. In this time of experimentation and research we saw steam engines, petrol engines, electric motors and gas engines, even hybrids and fully electric vehicles (the first electric vehicle was built in the late 1820s). The objective at the time was to find a fuel that was both efficient and environmental friendly, and electricity fit the bill. The first automobile to surpass 100 km/h (62 mph) was, in fact, electric – in 1899!

However, with time the focus of innovation shifted and standardization of fuel and infrastructure set in. Once the internal-combustion engine was seated as the dominant method of powering vehicles, baseline research on vehicular energy storage effectively ended for a century. Arguably, we haven't seen a *substantial* change in automotive propulsion since Gottlieb Daimler and Wilhelm Maybach invented the gasoline-powered internal-combustion engine for cars in 1885. Notwithstanding various iterations, including Wankel, turbocharged, supercharged and fuel-injected versions, the same internal-combustion process pioneered 130 years ago remains the beating heart of more than ninety-nine percent of our vehicles today. Correspondingly, petrol-unleaded and diesel fuels haven't changed much either, and we currently use 350 billion gallons of them every year.

The key to the success of the internal-combustion engine was primarily due to

- the abundance of fuel, i.e. the proliferation of a far-reaching infrastructure in support of it and
- its energy density, i.e. its ability to store huge amounts of energy in an easily transported form – which allowed the Model T a range of about 250 miles (which has remained the benchmark for desired range to this day).

Standardization has been good for growth and industry. Just like the common ground of Microsoft Word and PowerPoint software eases exchange of information between companies for over twenty-five years, so has a common energy storage platform been useful for the first century or so of personal transport. Common fuel and technology standards have allowed for incremental modifications, improving efficiency and adding power (such that 100 bhp per litre of engine capacity, unimaginable only 20 years ago, has become a rule today). Now, however, a new era of environmentalism, urbanization and innovation calls for something simply better than a combustion engine – by a number of measures. Like the last period of revolutionary innovation we need now to focus on a step-change that eliminates the errors and issues with the combustion engine, transforming twenty-first century transportation into a more powerful, far more energy efficient, cost-efficient and environmentally friendly solution.

Electric motors present the most credible, sensible solution to stopping (and ultimately reversing) the impact of climate change as impacted by transportation. These small cylindrical devices could also launch a new age of innovation and industrial enlightenment, and they represent enormous potential for growth – both attributes that governments are keen to be seen spurring on. Even Bob Lutz, former Vice-Chairman and President of Chrysler, former acting CEO of GM, and perhaps the auto industry's ultimate 'car guy' and 'petrolhead' noted: "The electrification of the automobile is a foregone conclusion."

Making precise projections as to when a revolution will take hold is a futile effort (if you were hoping to plot annual business strategy on the content of this book, I apologize), and it hangs in the balance of economic incentives, governmental steering, and social preferences. Certainly, the more advanced governments recognize this. In spite of the usual pre-election rhetoric on capping fuel prices, yet still supporting long-term innovation, some countries are successful in taking a longer-term political view.

Expressing targets (or wishes) and enabling them with funds is prudent. It's also consistent with nudge theory. Nicholas Short, Strategy Advisor for the UK Government's Office for Low Emission Vehicles, told me: "Governments around the world are clamping down on emissions and the UK is no exception. Our aim is for all vehicles in the UK to be effectively zero-carbon by 2050, and I think all vehicle manufacturers know they need to be investing in electric, fuel-cell, or hybrid technologies if they want to remain competitive." The government of Norway takes it a step further, and has aimed for zero emissions already by 2025. In any case, governments will not just gently encourage both users and manufacturers to tread the socially beneficial path of lowered emissions.

The nudge is not just with a stick, however. Mr. Short added that, in line with a stated goal to have every new car in the country an ultra-low emission one by 2040 (currently defined as under 75 g/km carbon dioxide emissions), the UK government has announced more than £900 million to support the market through 2020, providing funding for UK-based innovation and fostering national development of ultra-low emissions vehicle technology and infrastructure. With this, the UK aims to be among the world's leading markets for low emissions innovation – alongside California, Japan and Korea.

More than 8,500 charge-points are already installed across the UK today. The government has set in place a strategy that identifies the challenges it will face in carrying out the switch to electromobility, as well as tactics to overcome them. These include mandating zero-emission taxis (as of 2018 in London), changing traffic laws and motivating people to adapt to the change swiftly. The cost of driving into central London in anything other than an ultra-low emissions vehicle is currently £11.50 (close to $20), with greater fees levied for the highest-emission vehicles and penalties for non-compliance up to £195 (c. $330). This levy will continue to grow, creating massive disincentive for those travelling in anything other than electric vehicles or by public transport. These measures are proof of the government's commitment to changing the country's transport habits by 2050 – nominally for the betterment of the environment and the people, but also to achieve a more substantial political aim.

There is a greater political afterthought from promoting the use of alternative energies. Not only would such a move help curtail emissions and the occurrence of road traffic accidents, as well as improving transport systems in general, but on a national scale it would also help create fossil fuel-independent economies. By transforming a transport system the cost of importing oils can be significantly reduced (at the same time helping to alleviate major problems caused by air pollution), making governments keen to adapt. In the US, ninety-three percent of energy in the transportation industry comes from petroleum, according to the Edison Electric Institute. In 2012, the UK imported energy to the tune of £24 billion (c. €30 billion or $40 billion). By considering alternative power systems and storage for transport the dependency on a solitary form of (foreign) energy can be reduced. For the non-petroleum producing nations of Central Europe the need is even more pronounced than in the US (which since 2008 has been a net exporter of gasoline and is expected in 2015 to overturn its forty-year ban on exporting crude oil, amidst an abundance of fracking-generated fossil fuels).

When a country starts producing and storing its own transport energy there are benefits carried forward to consumers – the residents of the country. Specifically in the absence of fossil fuels, countries are looking for solutions to their energy problems from alternative sources. Ironically, while energy independence is a goal for governments, there is also a realization that finding the solution requires interdependence and collaboration – for both generation and the efficient and clean use of energy.

Simply put, we cannot clean one house on the street and expect the neighbourhood to win a beauty prize. If the entire planet is to be saved all nations will have to make a combined effort to reduce annual emissions rates. Hence

- the importance of the Kyoto Protocol; an international treaty on climate change that sets rules, obligations and limits on emissions of greenhouse gases in every industrialized country. This treaty was signed on the basis that industrialized countries are responsible for the climatic change, resulting from almost 150 years of industrial activity

- the agreement by EU lawmakers, announced at the end of September 2014, to impose a framework and deadline toward standardized electric charging points (i.e. common 'plugs').

While energy independence, energy use, emissions and standardization strategies and plans take years to execute, the first step is always accepting that a problem exists and that we need to look for a solution. Fortunately, we seem to have reached that point.

Electrification as the Solution

By helping to diversify our fuel mix, electric vehicles reduce petroleum dependence and tap into an energy source that's often locally generated and remains relatively inexpensive. Equally importantly, electric vehicles have the potential to unlock innovation and create new advanced industries that spur job growth and enhance economic prosperity.

In the long-term, electric vehicles are crucial to countries seeking to de-carbonize their transport sector. The International Energy Agency's '2DS' scenario (2°C Scenario) prescribes a future energy system that would limit average global temperature increases to 2°C by 2050. In this scenario the transport sector's potential share of overall carbon dioxide reductions would be twenty-one percent. In order to meet this target, three-quarters of all vehicle sales by 2050 would need to be plug-in electric of some type.

Sourcing Energy

Some cynics claim that electrification simply shifts the problem of fossil fuels to emissions caused in electricity generation (or, even more cynically, shifts profits from oil companies to energy providers). They claim it transfers the systemic pollution generated by creating energy in the first place from the point of use (i.e. a car in a city) to a less problematic place (i.e. power station sites).

While this might have been true a few decades ago, it's an outdated view today in most advanced countries.

Renewable sources today already account for almost twenty percent of the world's energy supply, with solar energy the fastest growing renewable source.

California's Pacific Gas & Electric generates around fifty percent of its energy from renewable sources (solar, wind, and hydro-power). Munich, for example, is aiming toward one hundred percent of the energy generated and used to be from renewable and environmentally compatible sources by 2025. No doubt many cities worldwide will follow suit.

It's not just a quality-of-life issue driven by tree-huggers in liberal cities, however – there's an economic incentive for utility companies as well. Forbes Magazine in August 2014 suggested: "Electric vehicles could save US utilities from a death spiral," adding that massive electrification efforts will drive demand, securing long-term growth. Electric production capacity – unlike oil – is currently levelled at peak-consumption. In other words, energy companies generally have as much capacity as will be necessary for the highest times of usage, as the cost of producing is still considerably lower than the cost of storing. Because of their batteries, electric vehicles are, in essence, also storage devices for energy and can be charged during times of low demand (while at home during night-time, for example). There is at the moment still little need to increase capacity, as long as charging is done during low demand (sub-peak) times – habits can be shaped by pricing measures. When charging takes place throughout the day, the peak energy requirements will increase. Both at micro-grid level (via batteries, fuel-cells, and thermodynamics), and at the home and office level (via lithium-ion batteries such as Telsa's Powerwall and SolarWatt's MyReserve), energy storage will allow for supply-side levelling without having to increase capacity at peak-demand times. This leaves energy companies with a 'win some, lose some' scenario, depending on their market position, either as energy generators or in energy storage.

Unlike fossil fuels, electricity is today generated at regional or local levels. Transmission of (and loss of) energy across wide swaths of land will surely fall as it can be produced at unit-level – in homes and offices via photovoltaic panels, fuel-cells, or even geothermic means.

So, what is true is that there will be a battle between energy and oil companies for the minds of the public. Each will seek for a position of maximum gain within the coming Mobility Revolution.

Massive investment from government and automakers alone won't suffice, however. In the same way that mechanical engineering was the key to the successful dominance of fossil-fuelled internal-combustion engines for 130 years, two fundamental elements will lead electric vehicles in conquering the next century of mobility. Both energy storage technologies and charging infrastructure must come together for our big changes to take effect.

The Electric Car, Part 1: Energy Storage and Range Anxiety

Chelsea Sexton was a specialist for General Motors' unsuccessful early-2000s electric vehicle programme who featured prominently in the 2006 movie *Who Killed the Electric Car*. She has since founded Plug-In America and the Lightning Rod Foundation – both are working to create the pre-conditions for a successful re-launch of electric cars in the US. Sexton believes that today things *could* be different, but nothing is guaranteed yet:

> "The current EV industry and movement shares more similarities and vulnerabilities with past efforts than most recognize. The main difference, however, is that there are more people and companies involved, and the public now believes electric vehicles to be 'inevitable'. The opportunities are huge, but so are the stakes. If the industry does not collectively follow through this time, there will be no excuses."

'Range anxiety' as a consequence of limited energy storage is considered the greatest hindrance to the adoption rate of electric vehicles. Mitsuhisa Kato, Toyota's Head of Research and Development, famously said at the beginning of 2014: "It will take a Nobel-Prize-winning battery before EV's go mainstream." Countering that, Volkswagen's Head of Powertrain Development, Heinz-Jakob Neusser, noted in a press-conference in October 2014 that at the current rate of development we should expect to see batteries that provide electric vehicles with a range of over 500 kilometers (310 miles) by 2020. In the meantime, he noted, plug-in hybrid vehicles (whether using the combustion engine for propulsion or as a range extending option for electric motors) fill a gap as an interim technology to appease consumers worried about the driving range of the vehicle.

I believe range anxiety is a bit of a farce, imagined out of a long-gone desire or Wild West fantasy where we get into our cars at any time and drive across the US. The classic American road-trip is never that spontaneous, however. (The one I took with friends from New York to California was planned months in advance and required at least two-dozen stops of at least 20 minutes each to fill the tank of our 12-mpg, late-1970s behemoth). When people are honest with themselves about how far they actually drive they may switch to battery-electric vehicles (either as a plug-in hybrid or a fully electric model) and realize that charging isn't so strange. After all, we have all become accustomed to charging our mobile phones every night too, haven't we?

Desmond Wheatley, CEO of Envision Solar, noted in an interview with Wired.com in October 2014: "The problem is we've got one hundred years of cultural norm that says I must be able to pull over somewhere, and I must be able to fuel in three to five minutes. That's what we've all be ingrained to think. I'm convinced that today's children will think it's hilarious that we ever pulled off the highway to charge."

The reality of how people use their vehicles is simply *different*. Most daily trips in the UK are fewer than fifty miles (80 km) in distance, whereas on the other side of the Atlantic roughly sixty percent of trips are over before reaching the thirty-mile mark (50 km). The range of most plug-in electric vehicles, such as the Nissan LEAF and BMW's i3, is actually sufficient for these trips and many Tesla owners may only need to charge up one or two times during the week, rather than daily. Hence, adoption of electric vehicles will take introspection and education in use as much as it will require innovative technology from scientists and engineers.

That said, Tesla has recognized the need to address range anxiety and made rolling out its proprietary Supercharger network on three continents a top priority. By June 2015, Tesla had installed more than 500 Superchargers worldwide; ninety-eight percent of the US population now lives within one hundred miles (160 km) of an outlet. Given that use of Superchargers is free, we can speculate that owners may even begin to use their car to charge their homes, rather than the other way around. Either way, it will be disruptive to electric companies.

Both Tesla and BMW are quick to point out that their respective (and as yet incompatible) DC fast-charging networks charge batteries to a substantial eighty percent capacity within thirty minutes. Drivers are still, however, reluctant to wait that long to charge their vehicles. As such it's promising to hear of a dual carbon project by Power Japan Plus called Ryden, which allows for charging at twenty times the rate of current lithium-ion batteries. While Ryden has been initially designed for laptop batteries, it's worth noting that Tesla cars run on exactly the same cells as a laptop computer (there are 6,831 of them in the Roadster), so the technology will surely be applicable. There'll be no more having to pencil in lunch while charging the Model S.

Going a step further, in August 2014 a research team at the University of Tokyo School of Engineering announced a new lithium-ion battery that holds seven times more energy than current hardware. Similarly, developers at the University of Alberta have used carbon in an innovative way to create batteries with an energy density five times greater than today's lithium-ion units. While this may or may not be worthy of a Nobel Prize, it certainly will help assuage grave concerns about the distance that electric vehicles can travel in the real world.

Tesla and Energy Storage

Alongside its global network of fast-charging stations called Superchargers, Tesla, with Panasonic, is investing in building a battery Gigafactory in Nevada. The Gigafactory will mass-produce lithium-ion batteries, setting a precedent for output from a single location. The $5 billion project will be completed by 2019, occupying more than five million square feet and allowing Tesla to create batteries at seventy percent lower cost compared to the batteries currently in the Model S sedan. What does that reduction mean? Estimates suggest that Tesla could pay $170-180 per kilowatt-hour instead of the current $400-500 (assuming the cost of lithium also falls with economies of scale).

The premise is simple. Currently half the total cost of Tesla's Model S is for the battery pack. By bringing battery costs down Tesla can subsequently lower the cost of future models (starting with the launch of the Model X and continuing with the Model III), allowing it to broaden its target market by increasing affordability. As a consequence, analysts have projected Tesla will sell up to 500,000 cars annually by 2020 (it aims to reach 100,000 units per year starting in 2015, making it – with only two products on sale – already a larger brand than Alfa Romeo and roughly at the level of Porsche in 2011).

By producing batteries at a lower cost than rivals, Tesla will provide itself with a competitive edge that others simply won't be able to match. Rather than keep the technology and the benefit to itself, however, Tesla is hoping that this reduction in costs will become a reason for competitors to seek collaboration in order to enjoy the benefits of the Gigafactory. Given the advancement of battery-electric vehicles built by European manufacturers in particular, it's likely that BMW, Daimler and others could become dependent on Tesla for much more than industry guidance and promotion of the electric vehicle agenda – they will need Tesla for its batteries.

The widespread adoption of electric vehicles – while increasing significantly – cannot be achieved with one broad stroke, or as a result of one watershed event. The transition will be a gradual one, and for the consumer it needs to be as 'painless' as possible. In other words, the incentives *and* the path of change need to be clear in order to make it easier for people to make the switch in not only their vehicles, but their driving behaviour as well.

Last but not least is the question of how energy is transferred to and stored within a vehicle.

The Electric Car, Part 2: Infrastructure

As mentioned, London already has more electric vehicle charging points than petrol (gas) stations, but the city is still keen to move forward. As of attaining approval in September 2014, French giant Bolloré Group is embarking on a nine-figure project to roll out a total of *6,000* charging (and car-sharing) stations in London. California has just over 1,800 charging stations as of August 2014 and continental Europe has in excess of 10,000 public stations already operational. PlugShare and ChargePoint have mapped 50,000 shared and 20,000 proprietary charging points, respectively, across the US. Germany's pledge to add another 1,000 to its current 2,900 charging points means it is finally making meaningful inroads against the 14,000 or so *filling* stations it boasts. In Germany, independent projects are contributing more than the government to building up infrastructure. Berlin-based

Ubitricity and BMW have each developed a concept whereby standard streetside lampposts can become charging stations, opening up the potential for thousands more stations and lowering the hurdle of installation cost. Beijing intends to use Ubitricity's technology to add up to 30,000 additional public charging stations.

Beyond public stations, most electric vehicles are sold or matched with private (home) charging stations. Just as file-sharing and WiFi-sharing has become a norm, many private charging stations will become public with peer-to-peer models emerging. Over 65 Tesla owners in the UK have already joined together under an independently-developed platform called 'TeslowJuice' to allow each other access to their personal, home charging stations; the Tesla owners can even find the stations via their onboard touchscreen and navigation systems. Similarly, openchargemap.org is an open source community of companies and individuals sharing charging station locations worldwide.

The most audacious plans are being put into place in China, however. In August 2014 China quietly began to arrange 100 billion yuan ($16/€13/£10 billion) in government funding to establish electric vehicle charging facilities nationwide. No doubt these charging facilities will spur further domestic developments in (national) electric vehicle infrastructure. (China has also stopped levying VAT on seventeen currently available domestic electric vehicles.)

The key role that governments and non-governmental organizations alike can play is to

- set an example by purchasing electric vehicles for governmental and public transport fleets (South Korean law, for example, dictates that twenty-five percent of all vehicles purchased by government agencies and state universities are electric; London and Barcelona have each mandated a switch to zero-emission taxi fleets within the next three years)

- issue incentives for the purchase of electric vehicles (Norway allows fully electric vehicles to drive in bus lanes and park for free in the cities, while owners are exempt from punitive road taxes, which for a time made the Tesla Model S the country's best selling vehicle)
- implement strong policies that support the development of infrastructure
- perhaps most importantly, educate citizens.

Through my consulting work in the automotive sector I have come across community and local governments keen to set an example by fielding fleets of electric or hybrid vehicles – often modifying or amending procurement policies for government contracts to explicitly accommodate a symbolic purchase. Similarly, London's commitment to replacing all of its buses by electric buses by 2020 (reinforced by a record order of 200 fully-electric BYD buses in July of 2015), sets a highly-visible example for the potential of electrification, and paves the way for wirelessly charging models that are already being tested in some parts of the world.

Buses are leading the charge (pun intended) in terms of wireless – or inductive – charging, which may prove to be the definitive answer to the range anxiety conundrum. In 2014 the British town of Milton Keynes launched a fleet of eight Street Lite electric buses that undertake a fifteen-mile route in the city. At the end of each route – coinciding with driver changes and passenger drop-off/pick-up locations – the buses wirelessly recharge their batteries to seventy percent capacity within ten minutes.

Competing with London, which like Milton Keynes also has trials underway for wireless charging, Berlin aims to be the first European capital city to regularly employ wireless charging when route 204 initiates inductive charging at the respective end-terminals in 2015. Similar technologies are already implemented in Mannheim, Germany, and Turin, Italy. In the US, the Utah Transit Authority has ordered a fleet of fully-electric buses from electric bus manufacturer Proterra with overhead units capable of supplying enough charge in ten minutes for a thirty mile (fifty kilometre) route.

Looking further ahead, a *dynamic* wireless charging infrastructure is being implemented along a seven-mile long (twelve kilometre) stretch of roadway by the Korea Advanced Institute of Science and Technology (KAIST) in Gumi, South Korea. The technology, which recognizes chargeable and non-chargeable vehicles, keeps the buses charged with eighty-five percent efficiency despite a gaping (at least in relative terms) seven-inch chasm between the road and the bus. According to Professor Chun-taek Rim:

> "Wireless electric cars, whether the technology is used to recharge parked cars or cars being driven, will facilitate the commercialization of electric cars. The technology is already the most promising solution, and it is expected to grow even more popular as battery capacity and price competitiveness improves." (*Korea Herald*, 13 August 2014)

The real advantage of wireless charging – besides not having to stop to refuel – will be the reduction in necessary storage capacity within buses and cars. The KAIST buses have batteries just a third the size of an electric car's battery, and the knock-on effects of less weight – slower wear to consumables is just one – are numerous.

Navigant Research estimated in February 2014 that: "Worldwide sales of wireless EV charging systems will grow from a few hundred in 2014 to nearly 302,000 by 2022," concluding that, "Features once considered luxury items, such as power windows and automatic garage door openers, tend to spread, over time, across all vehicle segments – and that is likely to apply to wireless charging, as well." Pre-empting a scenario where dedicated urban streets worldwide will be outfitted with inductive charging loops, Clemson University in South Carolina, Utah State University and the University of Auckland in New Zealand have respectively started work on test tracks that facilitate wireless charging (using technology developed by Bombardier, Qualcomm or Plugless Power).

Dr. Joachim Taiber, research professor at the Clemson University International Center for Automotive Research and chair of the IEEE Standards Association Industry Connections Activity in Electric Vehicle Wireless Power Transfer, confirms:

> "In-motion wireless charging is an interesting technical option for future generations of electrical vehicles to substantially increase their range capabilities via access to wireless charging infrastructure in the roads, while at the same time finding new package solutions to integrate the battery and the coil system in an optimal manner."

But will wireless charging become a widely accepted technology? Late in 2014 Starbucks began rolling out 100,000 Duracell Powermats that charge mobile phones wirelessly. The technology for this is neither prohibitive for Starbucks (the retail price of a Powermat is $120, or about €90), nor for the user (accessories to allow each phone to be charged wirelessly cost less than $25, or €20). Similarly, IKEA has already launched a full range of furniture that incorporates wireless charging. Effectively Starbucks and IKEA are bringing the concept of wireless charging to a mainstream audience (even beyond people who use an electric toothbrush!)

Since we know that Tesla's Model S essentially contains a few thousand moderately commoditized batteries, it's clearly no stretch to imagine wireless charging on our city streets in the same way Starbucks now has wireless charging in its coffee shops. So envision the scenario: while you pass through a drive-through to pick up your morning fix of skinny-soy-double-shot gingerbread latté, your car might just have received *its* morning shot of inductive energy – just enough in five minutes to get you to work and back.

The Scope of Electric Cars in Our World

As the figures on page 51 show, a considerable upswing in electrified vehicle sales (both fully electric and plug-in hybrid models) is expected in most countries and regions, with a corresponding increase in the installed base. The growth corresponds to an increase of available options and brands over the last few years. Roughly twenty electric vehicle models were available by the end of 2012, and by the end of 2015 another twenty or so will be made available globally (not including commercial vehicles, where electrification is only just the beginning). Notwithstanding a few failed product launches, it's a supply-driven market.

Norway currently leads the world in electric vehicles (including plug-in hybrids) sold per capita – fully one-third of new vehicle sales in the first quarter of 2015 were plug-in electric or plug-in hybrid vehicles; the government's aim is for 100% to be fully electric by 2025. The Netherlands follows with a healthy figure of 5.7 percent. As expected, China is quickly becoming a leading country in terms of electric and

Global EV Sales Penetration by through 2025

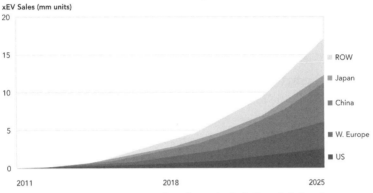

Source: Company data, FactSet, Morgan Stanley Research

Installed Base, EV And Plug-in Hybrids

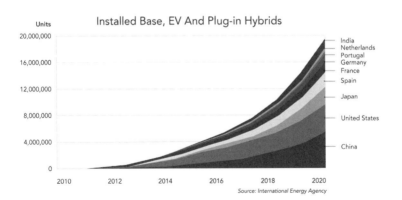

Source: International Energy Agency

plug-in hybrid vehicle sales by volume – by the end of the first quarter of 2015, close to 100,000 had been sold, the majority being pure electric vehicles, from local brands such as BYD, Kandi, Cherry and BAIC.

While in the US Chevrolet, Nissan, Toyota and Tesla dominated the rapidly growing market in 2013 and 2014, in Europe models from Renault, Mitsubishi and more recently, BMW have added to the mix.

Clearly, the widening supply of vehicles and increased choice will contribute to continued growth.

Electric cars are – perhaps surprisingly – simpler to build than their traditional counterparts. There is no combustion engine, no gearbox, no catalytic converter, no potentially explosive fuel tank and no customary transaxle. Maintenance is simple, too. There are no fluids (oils) to contain and no exhaust pipes to install. Beyond the (often third-party) supply of a

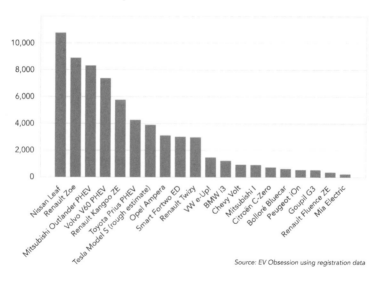

Europe Electrified Vehicle Sales 2013

Source: EV Obsession using registration data

Market Share of Plug-in Vehicles to Date in USA

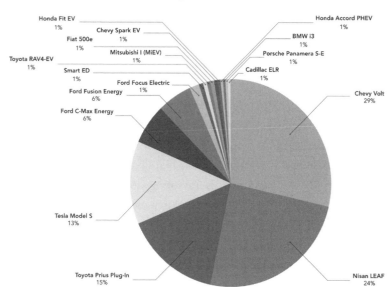

Source: Wikipedia, based on manufacturer data

battery and the electric motor, there is only the design and build process to take care of, which even then is easily (and often) outsourced, just as an iPhone is. In August 2014, a full-scale electric vehicle production facility was even offered for sale to subscribers of an electric vehicle group on LinkedIn, just as you might offer used DVDs on eBay.

All this means that many hurdles of entry to the automobile market are demolished and the field is truly open to new competitors of all sizes. Appearing in Chris Paine's 2011 movie *Revenge of the Electric Car*, Greg Abbott is a very resilient electric car converter based in Culver City, California. He has built, among other contraptions, a fully electric 1967 Camaro and a Porsche 356 Speedster. He's part of a movement consisting of independent electric vehicle converters, manufacturers and companies of various magnitudes. Via Motors, notably chaired by Bob Lutz, is a converter of commercial vehicles, building fully electric vans and trucks for fleet operators like FedEx, Verizon Wireless and Pacific Gas & Electric.

Fisker, Lightning Motors, China's BYD, Korea's LG, Croatia's Rimac, Turkey's Karsan, Tennessee's Shockwave Motors and Detroit Electric (like the Tesla Roadster, based on a Lotus Elise chassis) are the most notable of several dozen companies that have presented electric-vehicle prototypes, with the financial backing to grow. The Taiwanese producer of iPhones, Kindles, BlackBerrys and Playstations, Hon Hai Precision Industry Co. (also known as Foxconn), is investing approximately $800 million (€620 million/£500 million) in a manufacturing facility in northern China that will employ up to *100,000 employees* building electric vehicles priced below $15,000 for domestic and American markets. Some 10,000 of these vehicles are destined for a car-sharing scheme with Beijing Electric Vehicle (BEV). One might also expect Foxconn to produce electric vehicles for other brands as well (it already produces mobile phones for many brands).

Just as Daimler and Ford had their time during the first mobility revolution – an era in which hundreds of companies sought to produce horseless carriages (there were 272 brands in the US alone by 1909) – there will be a wave of electric vehicle pioneers, some with astounding investment and market power. As was also the case in the 1920s, however, this boom will be followed by a shakeout – something that will affect traditional automakers, too.

Although it generated 'only' $3.2 billion in revenues in 2014, I now consider Tesla (whose revenue Morgan Stanley expects will increase more than tenfold by 2016, thirty-fold by 2020 and sixty-fold by 2028) an established brand for electric vehicles. Among its piston-powered status-quo-abiding peers, these are the major players:

- General Motors, burned by their failure to properly market and sell the EV1 in the late 1990s, is still somewhat resolute in wanting to lead the way among American manufacturers (former CEO and Chairman Rick Wagoner has described killing the EV1 as his biggest mistake, although he also presided over the company when it fell into bankruptcy). They have blazed a trail by introducing the Chevrolet Volt (known as the Vauxhall/Opel Ampera in Europe) and the luxurious Cadillac ELR, albeit both with only limited initial commercial success. Despite mixed fortunes (strong sales on the US coasts, ambiguous in Middle America and discontinued in Europe), a sleek new-generation Chevrolet Volt will arrive for the 2016 model year with improved hardware including a stronger gasoline range-extender.

- Renault and Nissan (which are independent but operated as a group) are the bold electric vehicle pioneers in Europe, with the all-electric plug-in Renault ZOE and Nissan LEAF siblings each gaining a cult following. Luxury sister-brand Infiniti is also adding hybrid sport-utility-vehicles to its portfolio in 2015. The CEO of both companies, Carlos Ghosn (who has declared the merits of "zero emissions, zero particles, zero noise, zero oil"), has set upon a goal of selling 1.5 million electric vehicles by 2020 (although it should be noted that his initial deadline was 2016).

- Poised to lead the pack among the traditional premium manufacturers – albeit in different ways – are Daimler and BMW. Daimler has implemented Tesla's electric hardware into various existing models, including the B-Class, owing to the fact that until the end of October 2014, Daimler owned a five percent share in Tesla. By 2017, however, the German giant aims to have rolled out ten new models with plug-in hybrid technology, allowing even large cars such as the new S-

Class luxury limousine to achieve efficiency of more than 100 mpg (2.3 l/100 km). BMW, on the other hand, has committed to a full sub-brand: BMW i. Two models, the i3 and the i8, bookend the incipient marque, an i5 is getting ready for production, and a full palette, from i1 to i9 is conceivable. In addition, BMW intends to employ plug-in hybrid technology in every vehicle line in its entire range including in the legendary M-cars. The rivalry between Daimler and BMW ends at the charging station, however. They are now cooperating on a project developing wireless charging systems. This represents a sizable step toward expediting the pace of adoption of electric cars worldwide, as well as setting a standard for other companies that could help bring the technology to our streets earlier than first thought. BMW says the aim is to develop faster charging rates up to 7 kW (marginally beating WiTricity's announcement of 6.6 kW wireless charging).

- With its resolute launch and promotion of the Prius, Toyota has since 1995 become the undisputed leader in hybrid vehicles – even going so far as to ridicule solely electric vehicles in US in Lexus advertising campaigns (showing instead the benefits of hybrids). For most Americans, the Prius is synonymous with hybrid technology, although Toyota and Lexus already have a range of more than ten hybrid vehicles, covering most segments. Even while it is investing heavily in fuel-cells – a persuasive alternative to battery-electric storage, but more on that later – it remains strategically and financially committed to battery technology.

- In spite of the fact that Executive Chairman Bill Ford has been a prominent proponent of a green agenda within his own company ("They thought I was a Bolshevik," he said of his Board in 2012), Ford lags behind in defining a clear strategy for electric vehicle growth. "My fear is that we electrify the fleet and our impact is not what it could be,"

Ford noted at an industry conference in September 2014. Although Ford publicly insists that the company *could* build a Tesla-fighter, it currently offers only an all-electric Focus and two plug-in hybrids (the Fusion Energi and C-Max Energi). All three are based on existing gasoline models, compromising design and practicality. Ford *has* partnered with GE, however, to roll out WattStation vehicle charging stations to all its campuses across the US.

- Fiat-Chrysler – perhaps absorbed by their merger and late 2014 IPO – hasn't been an early leader in electric vehicles. Its modest small vehicle fleet, however, has so far allowed it to remain on the safe side of manufacturer emissions regulations. It offers an all-electric Fiat 500e, but barely stands behind it (CEO Sergio Marchionne said to an audience at the Brookings Institution in early 2014: "I hope you don't buy it because every time I sell one it costs me $14,000."). Nevertheless, together with a planned rollout of several fully electric and plug-in hybrid models, Fiat-Chrysler has turned its eye toward wireless charging, working together with NextEnergy (a nonprofit 'advanced energy catalyst' organization based in Michigan). Before wireless charging goes *underneath* the car, it will already be *in* some of Fiat-Chrysler's products; the 2015 Jeep Cherokee features an inductive charging unit for mobile phones in the centre console. Ferrari – to be spun out of Fiat-Chrysler in 2015 – has already launched the hybrid LaFerrari and 599 models.

- In the words of Canada's Globe and Mail, Kia (part of the Hyundai Group) will 'add Soul to the electric vehicle market' – a reference not just to their first fully electric model, the stylish Kia Soul, but also to the scope of the Group's ambitions in the electric vehicle market. Having already sold more than 200,000 hybrid vehicles, the Group is splitting its approach to the market by brands: Kia will sell both hybrids and fully battery-electric vehicles, aiming to be among the top-ten electric nameplates by 2016; Hyundai will sell fuel-cell vehicles and hybrids. In the pipeline are over twenty plug-in hybrid, fully electric and fuel-cell vehicles. Senior Vice President Lee Ki-sang, who heads the eco-friendly car divisions of both Hyundai and Kia, said at the launch of the Soul: "There is no clear direction about which eco-friendly cars will win."

- Volkswagen Group's strategy has been made publicly clear, is divided by brands, and is becoming progressively more varied and ambitious. Volkswagen itself offers the battery-electric e-up! and plug-in hybrids such as the e-Golf and the Passat GTE. The more luxurious brands in the portfolio – Porsche, Audi and Bentley – will focus on powerful plug-in hybrids. This division of labour is not set in stone, however, with the entire Group sharing technology. So far Porsche has announced that the legendary 911 will be hybridized and Audi has revealed the A3 and A6 e-tron models, the brand's first plug-in hybrids, for 2015 and 2016 respectively. Audi also intends to offer an entire range of electrified Q-series sport-utility vehicles by 2018. Beyond this, Volkswagen Group is hedging its bets for a broader electric future and aiming not to be outdone by Hyundai, confirming that more than twenty plug-in hybrid or fully electric vehicles will be available by 2020, with a special focus on China. It is also experimenting with fuel-cell designs. Like BMW and Daimler, with their venture-capital arms in the US, Volkswagen Group and the Piëch family hold a considerable number of non-integrated equity investments in long-term-future innovators.

No brand is exempt from experimentation. Rumours abound that Jaguar Land Rover are working on a plug-in hybrid Range

Rover; the company has also registered the trademark 'EV-Type', emoting the legendary Jaguar E-Type. At the 2014 Paris Motor Show Lamborghini exhibited the 900 hp plug-in hybrid Asterion concept, complete with a 5.2 litre V10 engine and three electric motors. If it comes as a surprise that Lamborghini built such a car, consider that McLaren has already blazed this trail with the 916 hp P1, and that the Porsche 918 – a car that holds the Nürburgring lap record for a production car – also employs the technology. (The fact that the Lamborghini would be officially rated at below 100 g/km of carbon dioxide emissions means, absurdly, that drivers would save on road tax and dodge inner-city congestion-charging zone payments, such as in London. Given the demographics of the Italian brand's typical client base, however, I suspect that saving money isn't the primary motivation to buy.)

Many innovations are happening outside of the manufacturers. Researchers at countless universities including UC Davis, Michigan Tech, TU Delft, RWTH Aachen, MIT and others are aiming to develop technologies better than what is currently on the market. McGill University in Canada, for example, partners Linamar, TM4 and Infolytica, and using current technology as a base their aim is to develop batteries with high energy-density for our next generation of zero-emission cars.

The Canadian Minister of State for Science and Technology, Gary Goodyear, announced a $4.7 million grant for the McGill University researchers from the Natural Sciences and Engineering Research Council's (NSERC) Automotive Partnership Canada Initiative. Partners of the initiative will provide a further $5 million in funding, helping expedite any future breakthroughs.

By developing drivetrains that are multi-speed, smaller in size and lighter, McGill researchers will be able to improve the performance of electric cars while reducing costs. This type of technology has not yet been used in mass-production road-going electric cars (although Formula E racecars have a five-speed sequential gearbox; more on these a bit later), but will put electric vehicles in an affordable realm for average earners, opening up a new target market solely for the companies involved in this initiative. The success of this project will also allow local and international governments to start planning an electric transport network for their own cities and states as adoption increases.

Next-generation batteries are of course the focus of many projects around the world. They will help solve the perceived range problem of the electric vehicle. Accepting that there is a minority of people who require a longer-range car, increasing the energy density of the battery is the obvious solution.

Last but certainly not least, two-wheeled motorists will be pleased to know that slates of motorbike manufacturers are lining up to build electric motorcycles.

Most notable is Harley Davidson, whose recent 'Livewire' prototype provoked a fair amount of outrage that was buried beneath a landslide of admiration and, even more so, curiosity. That a company with famously conservative clientele, who crave long days on the open road beyond the capabilities of current battery technology, has chosen to embrace electric propulsion is indicative of the incoming megatrend. Automotive soothsayers Navigant Research recently concluded that zero-emission motorcycles would sell to the tune of fifty-five million units between 2014 and 2023, with strong appeal to younger riders and small cargo delivery outfits.

Harley Davidson isn't the only established manufacturer preparing for the future. BMW has already launched an electric moped, the C Evolution, which has a range of sixty miles and top speed of 75 mph from a 49 hp electric motor. Honda and Suzuki have shown a range of concept bikes, too, spanning recreational use to urban commutes, but the new technology has also opened doors to newcomers.

US companies such as Zero and Brammo have won plaudits for their electric sports bikes. Journalists have been left impressed by the predictable handling traits of the bikes, their ease of use and, importantly, their effortless power. More so than most electric cars, electric motorcycles are a lot of fun, and their silent powertrains will surely be welcomed with open arms in suburban areas.

While removable battery packs that can be charged under the office desk or inside at home add convenience to ownership experience, range and price currently still hinder electric motorcycle sales. Motorcycles will benefit hugely from the same advances in battery energy density and cost that electric cars will enjoy.

Challenges to Widespread Adoption

With every major revolution comes several major challenges; this is the case with the shift from combustion engine to electric vehicles. Based on countless conversations with drivers, fleet owners, auto industry executives and journalists, the most significant hurdles besides range include

- the perceived performance of the electric car
- the perceived safety and reliability of the car
- the perceived cost of the car
- the major costs associated with electric car research and development
- the lack of urgency for a shift

The performance of electric cars doesn't stand alone – in the eyes of the consumer it will always be measured by the standards of internal-combustion predecessors. Perhaps because of the preponderance of 'tree-huggers' and environmentalists that adopted such cars early on, it's difficult for many to believe that, in reality, electric cars are *better* suited to real-world driving than their conventional vehicles. Car manufacturers are therefore keen to point out that when it comes to required range, 'silent' performance and the absence of changeable gears, electric motors can perform just as well if not better that what we're used to (one *Harlem Times* headline put it: "The BMW i3: Not Your Hippy's Green Car.")

Harking back to the days of Daimler and Ford, we have invariably used horsepower as a measure of performance of our cars. At the same time we've reveled in the 'overtaking power' and acceleration of this machinery, both of which are largely determined by a car's torque (measured in newton meters (Nm) or foot-pounds (ft lb)). Why should this make electrical vehicles superbly suited to our everyday driving tasks? Because electric motors have maximum torque from the outset – that is, instantaneously. Cars with an electric motor needn't reach a certain engine speed to generate the significant power required for forceful acceleration like internal-combustion engines do. What's more, they generate far more torque than traditional engines in terms of comparative size or weight. A Nissan LEAF (the world's most popular electric car) matches cars such as the Mazda 6, Honda Accord and even the BMW 320i in power with a motor the size of a shoebox.

Tesla goes further in illustrating the capabilities of the electric motor. With 310 kW (416 hp) and 600 Nm (443 ft lb), the Model S easily matches the power of the Porsche 911 Carrera S and surpasses both the Porsche and Ferrari 458 Italia in terms of intoxicating torque. The ferocious Model 'P 85 D' performance model takes Tesla's four-door sedan well into supercar territory, with a total of over 760 hp from two motors, allowing for 0-100 km/h (0-62 mph) acceleration under three seconds in 'Ludicrous' mode. The BMW i8 plug-in hybrid has broadly similar performance, reaching 60 mph in 4.2 seconds before hitting a top speed of 155 mph. Both the Tesla and the BMW generate but a fraction of the emissions of their purely fossil-fueled rivals (even when taking into account the energy-generation infrastructure), they can both travel more than 300 miles at a time, and they surely won't bore the average car aficionado. Even Jeremy Clarkson (*Top Gear* presenter and notorious EV-skeptic) couldn't help but fall for the i8, noting in his review (August 2014, *The Sunday Times*):

> "Wow. Toyota had just about convinced the world that if you wanted a hybrid, you could pretty much kiss goodbye to the concept of fun. But with the i8 BMW has shown this ain't necessarily so."

Perhaps that hedonistic drive in a roadster on a curvy mountain road doesn't have to be plagued with guilt after all…

Some people also need to be put at ease concerning the long-term safety and reliability of electric vehicles, as this impacts resale (residual) values of their car. Although electric vehicles have existed since the advent of motorized transportation, there continues to be distrust surrounding the technology, and in particular the new brands that are propagating it. People are often afraid to lose the money they are investing in a car, and without some kind of record detailing past depreciation many are doubtful of how dependable the technology is overall (the residual value of a Tesla Model S still needs to be ascertained, for example).

At an event where electric vehicle test drives were being offered, I listened and watched as prospective customers asked basic – almost absurd – questions about two Renault models.

Will it work when it's cold outside? Does the battery melt in the heat? Can I replace the battery en-route? Will the car explode in an accident? Will the fuses at my house support charging? Will the 120-mile range be sufficient for my daily twenty-mile commute to work, even if I stop off to go shopping? Will the car still work after three or four years? I admired the salesperson's patience, answering the same questions over and over, but it was patent that we've still got a way to go in winning over the masses about making a long-term commitment to an electric vehicle.

The risk of fire is one of the greatest fears surrounding electric vehicles. This apprehension is largely based on isolated incidents in 2011, which captured considerable media attention. Exhaustive testing has dramatically reduced the risk of such incidents, yet people remain doubtful. As Tesla CEO Elon Musk noted at a Dealbook conference in 2013 (subsequently cited in *Forbes Magazine*): "If fire risk is your concern, you'd have difficulty [finding] any better car than the Model S." He continued with some statistics that illustrate considerable media sensationalism and pro-establishment bias: "Tesla has had about one fire every 8,000 vehicles, compared to one in 1,300 for the industry average. There are 200,000 gasoline car fires every year. How many times do you hear about this [in the news]?"

Common sense seems to have taken a back seat here, too. As Musk puts it: "There should be absolutely zero doubt that it is safer to power a car with a battery than a large tank of highly flammable liquid."

Nevertheless, in order to increase sales of electric vehicles these suspicions need to be banished and considerable assurances provided that such incidents will not take place.

Beyond convincing drivers that electric motors can be fun, safe *and* environmentally friendly, education needs to assuage the perceived high cost of electric vehicles. This argument, too, is unfounded. Electric car devotees at conferences such as the annual Plug-In conference in California will attest that, given government incentives, reasonable leasing rates and cost-effective overnight home charging, we can effectively calculate that a US-bought Nissan LEAF has a two-year cost of around $1000. As of August 2014

- total leasing cost (24 x $199) $4776
- down payment, delivery and tax $4010
- federal tax credit for zero-emission vehicles   -$5,000
- fuel savings (based on 12,000 miles driven)   -$2,500

As Matt Stevens, CEO of electric vehicle consultancy Cross Chasm illustrates, the buying process needs to be put into the context of 'Total Cost of Ownership' (TCO), a concept that based on my own consulting experience fleet buyers are well aware of. End-buyers, however, sadly still don't fully incorporate it into their vehicle-purchasing process.

2014 Cruze 2LS	2014 Cruze Diesel	2014 Volt
$19,795	**$26,745**	**$35,422**
2014 Cruze 2LS	2014 Cruze Diesel	2014 Volt
$597/month	**$592/month**	**$527/month**
($236 car + $361 fuel)	($365 car + $227 fuel)	($419 car + $108 energy)

Source: Matt Stevens, Cross Chasm

Fully charging a Nissan LEAF or Renault ZOE costs less than a couple of pounds sterling (or euros; fewer than $3.00) – it is a negligible expense for most. Additionally, workplace and public charging solutions are often free. Nissan LEAF customers can charge for free for two years in the US while Tesla's Supercharger network is free for Model S drivers worldwide for the lifetime of the vehicle (something that won't change, we're assured).

Moreover, the lifetime maintenance costs of electric vehicles are significantly lower. Not a lot needs replacing or changing on electric vehicles and even the brake pads last longer, as the brake-energy recovery systems contribute to deceleration. All this may be another reason, of course, why your friendly neighbourhood auto-dealer is still a bit reluctant to sell you one; as you won't be back for a service at least until the tyres are worn, the revenue potential from regular maintenance is limited.

Taking into account purchase price (usually including generous tax credits), lower maintenance costs, fuel savings and low insurance rates, the Electric Power Research Institute estimates that plug-in hybrids and electric vehicles have a total cost of ownership saving of about ten percent versus comparable cars. Websites (such as this one, from the University of California at Davis: http://gis.its.ucdavis.edu/evexplorer/) will hopefully make it easy for consumers to calculate their own annual savings, if only they began to calculate on a TCO basis.

Still, the average Nissan LEAF owner (and certainly the typical Tesla owner) earns well into six-figures, indicating that the electric car is not yet seen as a 'primary purchase' vehicle. This may well change shortly, however. Tesla's Model 3 four-door sedan, due to launch in Mid-2016 as a 2017 model, is expected to sell for $35,000, putting it barely above the average price for a new car in the US ($31,250 in 2013). It will also have a strong range of 200 miles (360 km). Many analysts already view this as a game-changer for the industry, making

Tesla's technology accessible to a mainstream audience that will be prepared to buy it as a primary vehicle. The Motley Fool financial investing website compares Tesla's move to Apple's rise to dominance in the mobile-phone market, shifting from appealing to a small, niche-audience to dominating the market at large (which will make for interesting competition, given that Apple themselves are plotting entry into the market by 2020).

Again, growing the market toward the mainstream, in August 2014 Nissan and Mitsubishi announced a 50:50 joint-venture to build a small affordable electric car for the Japanese market. Priced at roughly $15,000 it would compete favourably with regular compact cars because of clear advantages in total cost of ownership.

The final factor inhibiting dominance and limitless growth for electric vehicles is the lack of *sustained* private-sector research and development investment that's required to continually improve cost efficiency and performance. The critical element is sustaining these efforts, as it gives consumers confidence in their investment. A fleet manager of over 1,000 vehicles, who had put some forty or fifty electric vans into his fleet in the late 2000s from Modec (a company that has since become insolvent), told me: "I got burned once – the next time I buy an electric vehicle will be when a well-known brand puts a long-term proposition on the table for us."

When General Motors (which has built more than 400 million vehicles in its time) killed its last electric car project in 1999 it failed to recognize that building a brand *and* educating a consumer takes multiple product generations – even more so when the brand or vehicle is charged with revolutionizing a 130-year-old industry. Revival marques (such as the new MINI and the Fiat 500) and upstart brands (such as Infiniti and Lexus) usually never earn a profit in the first product generation. Tesla, founded in 2003, only turned its first quarterly profit in

2013. Sustained investment is necessary to overcome trillions upon trillions of dollars of historic investment in the 'installed base' product – the internal-combustion engine vehicle.

In most cases a unique development approach needs to be adopted, requiring substantial detachment from previous efforts, in order to build upon current knowledge as well as experimenting with the unknown. By way of comparison: uninhibited innovators like Tesla are completely focused on delivering battery-only solutions, while traditional competitors are still encumbered by fitting electric vehicles into their traditional line-up (case in point, Ford). This means they are effectively joining the race for electric-vehicle leadership with a ball-and-chain of legacy technology tied to their axles.

I'm quite certain that it is baseline investment and an eye for *total* solutions that will decide which electric vehicle company becomes a leader in the technology in the next ten to fifteen years. Anyone can throw their hat in the ring for one-off solutions (case in point, Fisker).

Is it Urgent?

One last, key social factor hindering widespread adoption of electric vehicles is a general lack of urgency. Most drivers and consumers have – in their minds and their spreadsheets – always budgeted for the cost of energy (i.e. filling up their petrol vehicles) and simply accept as fact the impact that they are making on the environment. After all, if the oceans only rise a 2-3mm per year, that's not really a lot, is it? That doesn't really affect me, right? It does.

The projections on sea level rise are disturbing, based on real observations, and detrimental to coastal cities. We need to accept the critical nature of this transition concerning our continued quality of life on Earth.

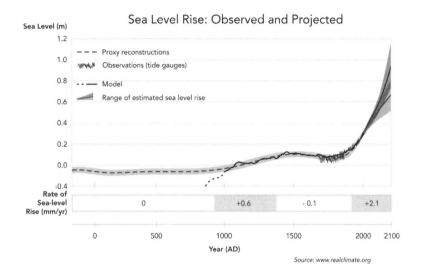

Source: www.realclimate.org

Alternatives to Batteries

Hugo Spowers is the founder and architect of Riversimple, a UK company designing and developing a hydrogen-powered vehicle for local transport needs. Passionate and convincing, Hugo's vision is not just to launch a fuel-cell vehicle, but to also revolutionize the vehicle ownership business model. Significantly, Riversimple is funded in part by Sebastian Piëch, a scion of the Porsche family, and joins a small but growing group of automobile projects using fuel-cells as a prime mover that includes Mercedes-Benz, Hyundai, Honda, BMW and Toyota.

Fuel-cells work much like batteries, releasing stored energy to power an electric motor. Rather than charging up with electricity, however, they refuel with compressed hydrogen at dedicated stations.

In June 2014 Toyota announced the development of its FCV, a purpose-built, fuel-cell vehicle subsequently unveiled at the influential Paris and Los Angeles Motor Shows and launched as the *Mirai* in 2015. Simultaneously, Toyota very publicly announced that it was ending its relationship with Tesla (Elon Musk had purchased Toyota's vacant car-manufacturing site in California in 2010 in exchange for a share of his company and the commitment to jointly develop an electric Toyota RAV4 and Lexus sport-utility vehicle). The announcement of the new fuel-cell vehicle in conjunction with a divorce from Tesla seemed to imply that Toyota was distancing itself from battery-electric vehicles. 24/7 Wall Street touted: "Toyota Bets Against Battery Electric Cars" in May 2014, and edmunds.com analyst John O'Dell was quoted in the *New York Times* saying: "It's obvious Toyota doesn't see a market for electric vehicles." Yet this is a very narrow view of the facts. Toyota continues to hold a $150 million investment in a lithium mining company in Argentina (which implies a commitment to battery technology) and builds a full range of different battery-electric and hybrid vehicles. Clearly, Toyota is hedging its bets and developing both alternatives, perhaps for different markets. As Shigeru Shoji, president of Volkswagen Group Japan noted, fuel-cell technology "may fly within Japan, but not globally." (Or, as one of my clients told me: "I've been in the business for over thirty years. Hydrogen fuel-cells have always been just five years away from a breakthrough.")

The crucial limiting factor for fuel-cells is infrastructure rather than technology. By the end of October 2014 there were fewer than 220 hydrogen filling stations around the world. In spite of Daimler and Linde's plan to roll out twenty fuel-cell stations in Germany 'in the coming years' and countless other examples of single hydrogen refilling stations being set up in cities like London and Los Angeles, the infrastructure commitment pales in comparison to electric charging stations and the ubiquity of electric power lines. Nevertheless, as fuel-cells are a uniquely efficient store of energy, I believe they will likely find use

- as range-extenders for commercial vehicles (Proton Power Systems, a German fuel-cell system developer, is working on solutions whereby hydrogen is produced on-board commercial vehicles in order to extend the range between charges, in theory, infinitely)
- in applications with a dedicated 'home base', such as construction sites, manufacturing facilities and airports. Airbus (together with South Africa's National Aerospace Centre) is even researching the use of fuel-cells for its auxiliary power units (APU) on commercial airplanes. Given then the possibility of a wider rollout of hydrogen storage units at airports, bus manufacturers will surely look into dedicated fuel-cell vehicles for airport use.

The applications of fuel-cell technology are not limited to vehicles, however, as the volume requirements can be as modest as a battery pack. At the end of 2014, Intelligent Energy, based in Loughborough, UK, began offering the Upp hydrogen-powered personal fuel-cell via the Apple Store. Using swappable hydrogen cartridges, the Upp claims to keep a mobile phone charged for one week. Conceivably, the same cartridge business model (familiar from razors and printers) could also prove to be a breakthrough for fuel-cells in automotive applications.

For wider applications there is also no reason why there shouldn't be even more and better options for storage in the future. Beyond lithium-ion batteries, lithium-metal polymer batteries (by Bolloré) and the fuel-cell, other energy storage alternatives are springing up. Swiss sportscar manufacturer

Quant will reportedly launch an electric sports car with a range of 370 miles and a top speed of 230 mph (365 km/h) fueled by electrolyte fluids. They are not alone – Michigan-based Sakti3 has similarly announced work on solid-state cells with electrolytes (Gatorade, anyone?).

There are others. The UK's Torotrack has developed a flywheel-based kinetic energy recovery system that stores energy through a flywheel the size of a large beach ball rotating at 60,000 rpm. Dearman Engine Company, based in London, is approaching zero-emission technology in another way still. Reviving a concept invented in 1899 in Boston, and sticking with a piston engine, the Dearman engine uses cryogenic liquid air (i.e. liquid nitrogen) as a store of energy that combusts in cylinders.

One litre of stored cryogenic liquid air is equivalent to roughly 700 times its volume in atmospheric air. When released, it rapidly boils and expands by seven times. This expansion is used to drive a vehicle with emissions solely of air. Liquid air is also a harmless, renewable clean form of energy, and as such is incomparable to any other form of energy. It seems the fuel comes without a catch – storing this kind of liquid energy to be used on demand is a unique concept that holds no small potential. Since it's stored at cool temperatures, it is also more efficient. Not only does this result in huge cost savings as well as fuel savings, but it also eliminates emissions of various pollutants earlier on in the supply chain, as well as at the end. Unsurprisingly, the tailpipe emission of a liquid air engine is, well, air.

Peugeot-Citroën has developed (albeit with no current intent to launch) a hybrid drivetrain that combines a small conventional internal-combustion engine with a hydraulic motor powered by compressed air. Using regenerative braking technology a pump continually refills an underfloor air tank that allows the vehicle to drive entirely on compressed air for short city runs. The system's chief benefit – besides the obvious ubiquity of the energy source – is the lack of necessary lithium-ion batteries.

So which technology will win? Well, it's not really a competition where only one finisher is the winner – several storage technologies can win. As Hugo Spowers says: "It's not an either-or battle for the future of the electric car. Both hydrogen and batteries can stand side-by-side at the filling-station forecourt." Just as today's filling station offers diesel, unleaded (at various octane levels) and natural gas, future filling stations will service hydrogen fuel-cells and batteries.

Nicholas Short, Strategy Advisor for the UK Government's Office for Low Emission Vehicles, in turn suggests: "Hydrogen and battery electric are at two different stages of development at the moment. The market for battery electric vehicles is clearly more established right now, but long-term there is conceivably a permanent market for both technologies. Those who need to drive from Edinburgh to London [for example] on a regular basis might rely on fuel-cells, with shorter-distance drivers opting for battery-powered vehicles." Deutsche Bank research auto-expert Eric Heymann in turn noted different *national* approaches in a *Manager Magazine* article published in July 2014: "Parallel infrastructures are conceivable, when and if different states pursue a different technological agenda."

Whatever the storage technology, I contend that electric motors are more efficient and fit more comfortably in keeping with the needs of today's (and tomorrow's) mobility than the internal-combustion engines they will eventually replace. They are ninety-five percent efficient in their conversion of stored energy into propulsion (compared to around forty percent for internal combustion engines), enable quicker acceleration, and require less packaging space than traditional combustion engines (whether they are diesel, natural gas, or gas/petrol). And the rush of adrenaline from all that torque makes them more entertaining – Tesla's Model S and BMW's i8 both evidence this indisputably. For now, battery-electric vehicles represent the least complicated path to adoption of cleaner transportation.

Electric vehicle racing – in Support of Positive Public Perception

With advances in hardware a number of electric car racing series have sprung up; some for profit, some to support the penetration of electric vehicles. The most prominent of these is Formula E, an open-wheel series supported by FIA, endorsed (to some extent) by the Formula One leadership and with considerable promise in innovation relevant to road cars.

Like any racing series, Formula E has its own set of rules, regulations and infrastructure, and it stands to grow in significance, relevance and impact. The series has partnered with BMW (the i8 is the official safety car), Aquafuel (even the generation of electricity should be clean, and Aquafuel generates it from algae) and Qualcomm (wireless charging is set to play a crucial part in Formula E from 2015).

As the inaugural season for Formula E came to a close in London in June 2015, no less than Sir Richard Branson noted, "I think four or five years from now you will find Formula E overtake Formula One in terms of number of people," adding that he too believes all new cars will be fully electric within 20 years' time. This is consistent with Formula E's ambitions. One of the leaders behind Formula E told me: "We truly want to leave behind a legacy in every city we race – a legacy of connected tracks, of wireless charging and of broad public interest in clean energy. The more people walk away from our races and believe in what electric cars can do, the better our world will be. In this sense, Formula E is a vehicle for saving our planet." It's an admirable objective and a bold statement for motorsport's contribution to environmental causes.

So even while some 'old school' racing fans decry the lack of snarling engines redlining at 18,000 rpm and the dizzying stench of racing fuel, thousands of new-generation race fans joined the pre-season festivities at Donington Park circuit in the British Midlands where the series is headquartered and subsequently turned out en masse for the inaugural race in Beijing. During the former some looked upon the electric vehicles (i3s, Teslas, ZOEs and LEAFs) that dotted the parking lot and pits with curiosity,

Formula E race at Donington Park circuit, August 19 2014;
photo: Lukas Neckermann

bewilderment and in some cases even spite (perhaps these were OEM employees fearing for their jobs); racing fans looked to the action on the track. One noted with approval: "This really is the future, isn't it."

True, the whirr and performance of 270 hp electric motors isn't as arresting as Formula One, but perhaps it is precisely this that will attract a new audience to motorsport. The complexity of the race is perhaps similar, but also different in that there is the additional real-world challenge of managing energy levels.

Next-generation drivers with familiar names (Senna and Prost), drivers with colossal experience (Sato, Piquet, Heidfeld and Trulli) and even a new gender in Formula-racing (with UK talent Katherine Legge) round off the picture for an exciting generation of motorsport.

Even FIA President Jean Todt, who is responsible for motor racing's ultimate competition, Formula One, is convinced. Just before Formula E's inaugural race in Beijing in September 2014, he noted: "For me the electric car is really the future of motoring in the cities."

Chapter 3:

Zero Accidents

" In the US alone 5.5 million road traffic accidents occur each year, with ninety-three percent caused by human error. **"**

Human-Driven Cars: Killing Machines in Disguise

Approximately 1.2 million people die in car accidents every year. Would we continue to travel by air if twenty jets crashed every day, killing everybody on board? In an editorial, British newspaper *The Sunday Times* writer Dominic Lawson calls cars "deadly weapons [that] travel at subsonic speeds and have wheels," and compares this "slaughter of young people" in our country to war in the Middle East.

In the US alone 5.5 million road traffic accidents occur each year, with ninety-three percent caused by human error (a similar proportion as in Europe). On top of the obvious dangers, the act of driving – single-mindedly steering a vehicle at a regulated, steady-pace along a highway or city street – has become an excruciatingly monotonous activity in a world where we are accustomed to multi-tasking at home or at work. As a result drivers focus on other activities and take great liberties in doing things simultaneously; texting, talking on the phone, fiddling with navigation systems and even worse. For some truly shocking insights on how desperately we need to let robots take the wheel ask a long-distance truck driver – who sees it all from above – about what he or she has witnessed people doing while behind the wheel.

Distractions, poor judgment and alcohol are leading factors in automobile accidents, with an annual economic cost of $300 billion, according to the Eno Center for Transportation. Robots programmed to undertake tedious repetitive activities address these issues (they also tend to be teetotal). In cities such as Barcelona, Copenhagen, Paris, London, Budapest, Sao Paolo, Seoul, Tokyo and Hong Kong, and at more than a dozen airports in North America as well as various Disneyworld sites, millions of people are already efficiently and safely transported from one place to another by driverless trains. Recognizing this helps us to overcome the notion that we are somehow more capable than machines at standardized tasks like driving to work.

Even with traffic laws forbidding the use of mobile devices while driving, as well as eating behind the driving wheel, somehow the severity of the situation eludes us. More than one million deaths every year is no laughing matter; stern action must be taken, and it can be. It is not that more stringent laws are required – no one wants to crash and the vast majority of people value their lives more than any fee they would have to pay. However, that humans continue to drive while drunk and distracted indicates to me that, relative to robots, we are not always capable of making the right choices under pressure.

For many people the gut reaction to driverless cars is distrust and denial: 'No robot could ever do what I do on the streets'. Yet we accept that robots are able to make pre-programmed decisions more quickly and efficiently than humans in other areas of our lives. We know that they are more proficient and exacting in manufacturing facilities. We use them in one form or another whenever we order goods online. We have even started accepting them into our homes, letting them loose as we sleep – iRobot and Dyson each make vacuum-cleaning robots that suck up our mess overnight. Even dairy farmers – a rather conventional demographic – have come to accept that milking cows and filling up milk bottles with their bare hands takes too much time in comparison to an automated system. In the meantime, every movement in the process has become computerized and is performed to perfection (as per a survey of 1,000 cows…). Similarly, large-scale farmers have also accepted autonomously-driving tractors to plough fields (John Deere, Fendt and Case all offer such machines). Perhaps we can learn to embrace robotics like our rural friends?

As Marc Andreesen, founder of Netscape and venture capitalist, tweeted in June 2014: "Self-driving cars and trucks are a moral imperative." While the bulk of our conscious decisions during driving are in reaction to judgments made when we encounter turns or events, the self-driving car is designed to already know every turn and obstacle that is ahead of it. This car will not make errors of judgment because of distractions the way a human driver does. It will not take as long to make crucial, split-second decisions as humans do, either. It will likely not be busy in chatting with other cars about what to make for dinner and how Tom was late for school this morning. Simply, machines do not need to sleep, eat, chat, or indulge in any other activity like we do while we repetitively turn left, right, stop, or accelerate. That makes them ideal chauffeurs.

So why don't the aforementioned twenty jets crash every day? Because of well-trained pilots who are able to recognize their limits and willingly cede the pleasure of flying to the autopilot systems, understanding that the vast majority of air catastrophes in the last two decades have been due to human error. Ask a pilot how much flying they *have* to do and how much they actually *do* and they will generally (and a little begrudgingly) tell you that the computer systems are able to control the airplane at any airborne point right through to landing. Even the steering wheel was removed from the cockpits of most commercial jetliners a long time ago (replaced by joysticks) and most accidents that do occur are during taxiing.

Perceptions on the need for human intervention in driving are changing, however. One participant in a KPMG focus group on self-driving cars noted: "I would trust that car more than I'd trust a bus driver in Manhattan. I'd trust that car more than I'd trust myself. I think the technology is much more intelligent than I am." (Reported in a 2013 study *Self-Driving Cars: Are We Ready?*)

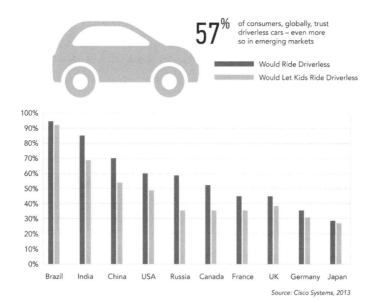

Source: Cisco Systems, 2013

Value-Proposition: Time, Efficiency and Enablement

The value-proposition for autonomous vehicles goes well beyond saving lives. For a country's economy to be sound an efficient transport system is crucial. Transport systems are the arteries through which the lifeblood of commerce flows. With increasing urbanization the need to develop a better transport system before collapse sets in is paramount. Liken it to making the choice to reduce cholesterol to prevent a heart attack. As most businesses depend on a structured and efficient transport system to deliver services to their customers, governments also need ever-improving traffic solutions; the economic consequences of traffic jams amounts to €100 billion ($130 billion) in the EU alone.

Individuals in traffic jams collectively waste four billion hours every year in the US alone. The average commuter in China spends five hours on the road each day (not counting the famed one hundred-mile traffic jam that took eleven days to clear in 2013). In turn, the abovementioned KPMG focus groups enthusiastically noted the shorter commutes and additional productivity that autonomous cars would afford them. Given the overwhelming benefit, even passionate drivers exhibit an overwhelming willingness (eight out of ten, no less) to use self-driving cars. The key factors were time saving, ease-of-use and the ability to regain control of the vehicle when (or if) the desire arises.

Increased value isn't limited to farm tractors and road-driving automobiles, either. Combining the safety and efficiency of its armed forces, the US Congress has set a goal for one-third of all combat vehicles to be autonomous by 2015, an intention that originally fueled the so-called DARPA (Defense Advanced Research Projects Agency) Challenge. Just as military projects have historically led to significant advances in navigation, so too did the DARPA Challenge focus the minds of robotics engineers, including Sebastian Thrun and Chris Urmson from Stanford and (originally) Carnegie-Mellon University, respectively.

In February 2011 Sebastian Thrun (who had at that point become the head of Google's self-driving car project) made a presentation at a Technology, Entertainment, Design (TED) conference, where he gained considerable notoriety for showing how self-driving cars will enable millions of visually-impaired people (and surely many more motion-impaired people) to gain new freedoms. Thrun, who told the audience he had dedicated his life to finding the solution to car-accidents after losing his best friend to a car accident at the age of eighteen, became the symbol of the autonomous-car revolution. His video has been viewed more than two million times on YouTube and has given perspective, not to mention hope, of new mobility for disabled non-drivers all over the world.

Similarly, the elderly stand to benefit. In the KPMG study Hank, a seventy-year old affluent focus-group participant, indicated that self-driving cars are exactly what he's looking for: "If I could have someone do all the driving for me, that would be fine." Regarding driving, he said: "It's work now." Most tellingly, Hank indicated that he'd be willing to pay a fifty percent premium over the average price of a car were it autonomous.

We'll go into each of these benefits in greater detail in this chapter.

An Overview of the Future Car, Today

In his 1953 short story *Sally* Isaac Asimov predicted a world (in 2057) where only 'automatics' – what he called autonomous cars – would be allowed on the road. The story's protagonist writes:

"I can remember when there wasn't an automobile in the world with brains enough to find its own way home. I chauffeured dead lumps of machines that needed a man's hand at their controls every minute. Every year machines like that used to kill tens of thousands of people. "We take it for granted now, but I remember when the first laws came out forcing the old machines off the highways and limiting travel to automatics. Lord, what a fuss. They called it everything from communism to fascism, but it emptied the highways and stopped the killing, and still more people get around more easily the new way."

Sixty years later self-driving cars no longer seem like something we would see in a science-fiction movie, where orbs are ferrying spandex-clad denizens to their destinations through the sky. Google's self-driving car is already on the roads of Nevada and California and most major manufacturers have announced plans to release cars onto the market within a few years. The era of self-driving cars and trucks is close at hand.

Let's look at the various levels of aptitude of an autonomous vehicle. (There are numerous interpretations of these levels; some reports call for three levels while the Society of Automotive Engineers (SAE) talks of six levels of automation. I'll focus on the more commonly accepted four-level definition).

- Level One autonomy – called 'function-specific automation' – is basic automated controls such as can be seen in virtually every one of today's vehicles. Actions include cruise control, lane guidance and parking sensors. In this form of autonomy the driver is aided by machines for some basic tasks but maintains overall control of the car. Most reports indicate that this low level of automation will effectively be obsolete by 2025 or 2030, as higher levels become ubiquitous.

- The second level – called 'combined-function automation' and becoming more common in some modern cruise-control systems – takes automation a few steps further, with major controls and actions performed by the machine. This level includes 'traffic-jam assist' or 'stop and go' features that adapt cruise control and keep the car centred in its lane. Many current models by Mercedes, BMW, Volvo and even Cadillac can be considered full Level Two automated vehicles. Here the machine handles some tasks, however the driver needs to be present and attentive in order to take over driving when the need arises. In most cases the driver can stay disengaged until prompted by the car to take over.

- The third level of automation includes self-driving features and takes control away from the driver to the point that he or she doesn't have to pay any attention to the road at all. Some cars today feature fully autonomous parallel parking (offered since 2014 on various Volkswagen, BMW, Lincoln, Toyota and Ford models), where the car measures the parking spot and guides the vehicle in. However, at some point the driver might have to take over if the car deems the situation 'unworkable'. A reporter with Germany's Auto Bild magazine in late 2014 drove a Mercedes C220 (with all available Autopilot options) for 965 kilometres (about 600 miles) from Flensburg to Füssen, only rarely aiding the steering wheel and twice applying the brake pedal. With current technology, the Mercedes could arguably be considered a Level Three autonomous vehicle, were it not for sensors in the steering wheel mandating some sort of contact (the reporter used a banana peel).

- The ultimate form of the autonomous vehicle is a car that doesn't need any input from passengers, other than perhaps to define the destination. Examples include the City Mobil public transport vehicle now being investigated for rollout in select urban areas and the UK Autodrive consortium vehicles that will be tested in Milton Keynes and Coventry from 2015. When we have reached mass implementation of this level of autonomy, parents could place their children in the self-driving pod for the daily school-run or trip to sports practice and then get in their own PRT and head to work.

With all that in mind, how does vehicular autonomy save lives? Perhaps most importantly, self-driving vehicles use a decision-making system that is based on solid facts – devoid of any emotions – to avoid getting into dangerous situations in the first place. They are utterly objective. Alexander Mankowsky, future trend researcher at Daimler, opined in an interview (Frankfurter Allgemeine Sonntagszeitung): "A robot-car simply wouldn't overtake on the wrong lane or drive over red lights." He added that if situations did become dangerous then 'robot-cars' would do everything possible to minimize the injuries or death toll.

Nevertheless, if, for example, a drunk driver does swerve and is about to crash into an autonomous vehicle the robotics will be able to gauge its next move by analysing the road and surrounding vehicles before quickly devising then executing an appropriate course of action based on a greater source of data than any one driver could ever access. In the event of car-on-car collisions, one of the main aspects in deciding the right course of action involves determining which vehicle is capable of absorbing energy from an impact with the least amount of damage.

Fully autonomous vehicles are simply programmed to make better decisions when faced with hazardous situations. Indeed, a car that is driven by 'thinking' software is far more likely to choose a course of action that might save lives than a car driven by a human who (over-)reacts instinctively, late and perhaps selfishly.

Late in 2014 on the famed Hockenheim racetrack in Germany, Audi raced an autonomously-driven RS7 against an otherwise identical, human-controlled RS7 at speeds up to 300 km/h (190 mph). The autonomous vehicle won by over five seconds.

How Demographic Trends Support Autonomy

Changing demographics support self-driving technology. While many of us grew up with the notion of a car and a driving licence being the equivalent of freedom and status – former British Prime Minister Margaret Thatcher famously said: "A man who, beyond the age of twenty-six, finds himself on a bus can count himself as a failure" – studies indicate that younger generations are not particularly interested in driving. After all, for millennials it would mean that they have to stop texting (Facebook-ing, Snapchat-ing and Whatsapp-ing etc.) and actually pay attention to the road. Accustomed to multi-tasking, this aspect of modern society nevertheless raises questions as to how committed they would be to driving without distractions and whether their behaviour behind the wheel is similar to their conduct in the lecture halls and classes.

In 1978 roughly half of youths attained their driving licence upon reaching the age of sixteen and seventy-five percent of seventeen year olds had passed their driving test. In 2008 only thirty-one percent of sixteen year olds and forty-nine percent of seventeen year old had licences in the US. These figures evidence a clear trend, with the millennial and 'digital native' generations preferring to spend their time involved in virtual and real social settings instead of behind the wheel. The iPhone has replaced the 'first car' as the primary object of desire for sixteen to eighteen year olds; sadly correlated, texting while driving has also become the leading cause of death among teenagers in the US.

Younger generations total 133 million potential drivers in the US; current drivers account for forty-three percent of the total population.

At the other side of the age spectrum more than forty million adults in the US are aged over sixty-five years and many do not drive due to mobility issues. In China, while still younger on average than most of Western Europe, fifteen percent of the population – or roughly as many people as the total population of France, Germany and Italy combined – will be over sixty-five years old in 2020. Clearly, 'seniors' are an attractive demographic.

What about the majority of drivers who fall between these two age groups – between those who are young and unwilling to drive and those that are too advanced in age to be able to (safely) operate a car's controls? Many current car owners have accepted that they would willingly give up driving if presented with a better option.

Lastly add people with limited economic means, who today rely on public transportation but tomorrow may rely on its equivalent – shared autonomous vehicles – and you effectively have the *entire population* as the target market for self-driving cars. This is in stark contrast to the existing target market of the automotive industry and suggests enormous potential for self-driving vehicles. Anyone estimating the scope of autonomous vehicles by extrapolating from the size of the current automobile market will fall woefully short.

Just as autonomous vehicles will open up new opportunities for the automotive and mobility sectors, they will also lead to growth in other industries as well as increases in GDP contribution. A more philanthropic consequence is that they open up a world of opportunities and travelling for people who suffer from any sort of disability.

So How Long Will it Take and What Will the Impact Be?

Adam Jones, automotive analyst at Morgan Stanley, is perhaps most bullish on the technology. He enthusiastically notes that the combination of autonomous vehicle technology and drivetrain electrification will create a utopian world, with one hundred percent autonomous vehicles sold, starting in 2026. In a research report he also notes the link to efficiency: "Autonomous technology takes fuel efficiency to entirely new levels, ultimately making a 100-mpg internal-combustion engine vehicle an attainable goal." Jones thinks that autonomous cars will contribute $5.6 trillion in annual economic savings globally. In October 2014 Morgan Stanley doubled-down on their predictions and announced that autonomous vehicles will lead to the death of the traditional auto industry (along with the traditional auto-analyst) in less than fifteen years' time.

Is this projection realistic? Perhaps – if we view autonomous vehicles in the context of other significant safety developments and compare it to the rollout speed we're accustomed to from the software industry.

The seat belt, which has reduced traffic fatalities by fifty percent, didn't become mandatory for use in most US states until the mid-1980s, roughly a century after the invention of the automobile. The first automatic transmissions were developed in the early 1930s. However, they took almost fifty years to become affordable for the mass market; now they are the inevitable standard in most cars of today. Likewise, the airbag was first introduced in 1973 as a very expensive option perceived as being unsafe at that time (after all, who wanted a bag exploding in their face?). It took a further twenty-five years to become a common technology, nudged on by a combination of government mandates and affordability induced by economies of scale. Hybrid vehicles, such as the Toyota Prius, which went on sale in Japan in 1997, have clearly gained acceptance in some markets over time (over a quarter of all vehicles sold in Japan are hybrids), yet today total sales of hybrid vehicles remains below five percent in most markets.

In light of this trend we'd usually predict that self-driving technology would become 'normal' only by 2040 or 2050 – a timeframe also predicted by most countries. Based on traditional innovation cycles and needs, many believe that over the next twenty to thirty years the self-driving car will undergo numerous major performance tests and improvements so that by the time the people are ready to make the shift the technology is ready, too.

I tend to disagree. Perhaps the quickest – and so far among the most significant – technological rollout in the automobile industry was electronic stability programming (aka ESP, DSC, VSP, or stability assist), which was first launched by Bosch together with Mercedes-Benz in the 1995 S-Class. Just two years later it received unplanned global recognition. When a new entry-level Mercedes-Benz A-Class failed a stability manoeuvre (known as the 'moose test') undertaken by a Swedish car-magazine, ESP was quickly implemented as a standard solution for the model. Mercedes thus launched ESP technology onto the mass market and forced all of its competitors, in all classes, to expedite their own rollout plans. Within a decade most new cars launched by European manufacturers offered ESP, with fifty-eight percent of consumers opting for it. To further nudge adoption, the EU, Canada, the US and Australian governments mandated that all new models sold after 2011 include the software as a vital safety feature. In other words, ESP effectively penetrated all new vehicle sales within sixteen years of its launch in the Mercedes-Benz S-Class.

The impact has been dramatic. The National Highway and Traffic Safety Administration (NHTSA) calculated that the widespread rollout had reduced accident rates by roughly 10,000 annually in the US (presumably most of the remaining incidents are not caused by driver error).

I suggest that the adoption of autonomous technology will tread a similar path to the adoption of ESP, perhaps even exhibiting the speed of typical changes in the computer industry. Moore's Law, named after Gordon Moore, co-founder of Intel, states that computer hardware performance roughly doubles every two years. As Microsoft-founder Bill Gates famously said: "If GM had kept up with the technology like the computer industry, we would be driving $25 cars that got 1,000 miles to the gallon." Spurred on by the pace of change and innovation, the adoption of software-driven technology is simply faster: it took close to forty years for eighty percent of US households to have electricity, twenty-five for eighty percent to have refrigerators, twenty for eighty percent to have mobile telephones and it will take fewer than ten for the same proportion to own smartphones (Asymco data, 2014). Given that an autonomous vehicle's safety benefit is to eliminate fatalities – aligning the interests of government, industry and consumers – we should expect penetration rates and speeds similar to the smartphone. I am convinced that at least fifty percent of new vehicles sold in industrialized nations will be equipped for Level Three or Level Four autonomy by 2020.

What about self-driving public transport? London Mayor Boris Johnson's 2050 transport plan initially included replacing driver-operated buses with driverless ones. The plan was introduced on the premise that structuring a transport system consisting of autonomous buses and vehicles will not only make London more efficient, but will also provide cost-cutting opportunities. His statements were quickly retracted under union pressure when attention was brought to potential job losses, but it should be expected that the plan will go through, and sooner rather than later. A similar arrangement was implemented when the Docklands Light Railway was implemented. The DLR, as it's known, now operates without human intervention.

Similarly, UK Business Secretary Vince Cable has announced a review of the laws that make driverless cars illegal and has paved the way for testing in at least three cities in 2015. The British Government has also set aside a fund of £20 million to support research and development in this area.

Since the end of 2014, California has permitted autonomous vehicle testing to a number of manufactuers including Google, Tesla, Apple and others; other states and countries have followed suit. Mercedes is now allowed to test its self-driving 'Future Truck' on highways in Baden-Württemberg, Germany.

Who is on board?

So, given my prediction in the last section, when do the big companies say we'll be able to buy a driverless car? Google, naturally, is most optimistic. In 2012 Sergey Brin committed to bringing a driverless car to market by 2018, given that

- California has already permitted driverless vehicles on its own streets (see permit on page 94)
- prototypes of the Google car are already on public streets and

OCCUPATIONAL LICENSING BRANCH
AUTONOMOUS VEHICLE TESTING (AVT) PROGRAM
TEST VEHICLE PERMIT

PERMIT EXPIRATION DATE

NOTICE: This permit must be kept in the vehicle or in possession at all times when operating an autonomous vehicle.

09/15/2015

SECTION 1 — TYPE OF VEHICLE

✓ Auto   Commercial

VEHICLE IDENTIFICATION NUMBER	LICENSE PLATE NUMBER	MAKE	YEAR MODEL
		AUDI	2012

SECTION 2 — MANUFACTURER INFORMATION

MANUFACTURER NAME	AVT NUMBER
VOLKSWAGEN GROUP OF AMERICA INC.	AVT001

BUSINESS ADDRESS
2200 FERDINAND PORSCHE DRIVE

CITY	STATE	ZIP CODE
HENDON	VA	20171

SECTION 3 — ACKNOWLEDGEMENT

The autonomous vehicle is being operated on roads in this state solely by employees, contractors, or other persons designated by the manufacturer of the autonomous technology.

The autonomous vehicle has a mechanism to engage and disengage the autonomous technology that is easily accessible to the operator.

The autonomous vehicle has a visual indicator inside the cabin to indicate when the autonomous technology is engaged.

The autonomous vehicle has a system to safely alert the operator if an autonomous technology failure is detected while the autonomous technology is engaged, and when an alert is given, the system shall require the operator to take control of the autonomous vehicle or if the operator does not or is unable to take control of the autonomous vehicle, the autonomous vehicle shall be capable of coming to a complete stop.

The autonomous vehicle shall allow the operator to take control in multiple manners, including, without limitation, through the use of the brake, the accelerator pedal, or the steering wheel, and it shall alert the operator that the autonomous technology has been disengaged.

The autonomous vehicle's autonomous technology meets Federal Motor Vehicle Safety Standards for the vehicle's model year and all other applicable safety standards and performance requirements set forth in state and federal law and the regulations promulgated pursuant to those laws.

The autonomous vehicle has a separate mechanism, in addition to, and separate from, any other mechanism required by law to capture and store the autonomous technology sensor data for at least 30 seconds before a collision occurs between the autonomous vehicle and another vehicle, object, or natural person while the vehicle is operating in autonomous mode. The autonomous technology sensor data shall be captured and stored in a read-only format by the mechanism so that the data is retained until extracted from the mechanism by an external device capable of downloading and storing the data. The data shall be preserved for three years after the date of the collision.

SECTION 4 — CERTIFICATION

I certify (or declare) under penalty of perjury under the laws of the State of California that the foregoing is true and correct.

PRINTED NAME	TITLE	AREA CODE/TELEPHONE NUMBER
		( )

SIGNATURE	DATE
X	

NOTICE: This permit enables the above described vehicle to operate in the capacity as an AVT vehicle.

ISSUING OFFICE	DATE
HQ R-1	09/16/2014

ISSUING EMPLOYEE'S PRINTED NAME	ISSUING EMPLOYEE'S SIGNATURE
ANNE FRENCH	X _Anne French_

OL 313 (NEW 9/2013) UH

Test vehicle permit

- research suggests consumers are more likely to trust software companies with the development of autonomous vehicle technology than traditional automakers.

This clearly doesn't seem far-fetched. As British magazine *Auto*

Express noted (June 4th 2014), the ambition is greater still. "Google isn't making a car; it's making an automated taxi cab." The Google car is indeed designed to be summoned by a smartphone app and to drive us to our locations autonomously. It doesn't have a steering wheel but it does have full and constant 360-degree 'spatial awareness' (which is more than can be said for even the best human drivers).

What then is the status quo in the automotive industry? Every manufacturer of relevance is working on some autonomous driving features, and CEOs of various companies have committed to a range of dates. Here are the leaders:

- No traditional manufacturer has stretched itself further than Volvo, which has proclaimed a clear goal that there should be no fatalities in its vehicles by 2020 (for decades it has also forensically analysed every accident involving one of its cars within a sixty-mile radius of its Swedish headquarters in an effort to better understand how it could have been avoided.) "Volvo Cars' long-standing human-centric approach and commitment to safety gives us a different starting point from other car manufacturers when we address the field of autonomous driving," says Håkan Samuelsson, CEO of the Volvo Car Group. The company's 2015 XC90 includes adaptive cruise control (ACC), like Mercedes-Benz's S500, and will add steer-assist. Furthermore Volvo, like Google, will test its own one hundred-strong fleet of autonomous vehicles in its hometown Gothenburg. It wants to sell self-driving cars to the public by 2017.

- Volvo Trucks also offers adaptive cruise control, lane-change support and driver-alert support, making its commercial trucks considerably safer. The next step is for the vehicles to communicate with each other (dubbed 'V2V') in a move toward autonomous convoys (imagine thirty to fifty trucks in sequence, like unhitched trains but on the highways). A chain of four Volvo trucks has already been tested in this manner, at speeds of 55 mph with considerable efficiency benefits (due to the aerodynamic principle of slipstreaming).

- After Volvo, Renault-Nissan is most buoyant on the future of Level Three and Four autonomous vehicle technologies. Carlos Ghosn told reporters at the 2013 Detroit Auto Show that by the end of the current decade autonomous vehicles would be "ready for prime time." Andy Palmer, then Executive Vice President of Nissan USA (and now CEO of Aston Martin) confirmed that Nissan would make fully autonomous vehicles available to the consumer by 2020 – a pledge many other manufacturers have begrudgingly had to match.

- Daimler CEO Dieter Zetsche has become very bullish on autonomous technology. In recognition of the threat from non-automotive competitors, he announced collaborations with both Apple and Google in 2015, declaring, "We don't want to become contractors... supplying hardware to third-parties." Mercedes-Benz is quietly busy implementing various elements of autonomous technology – it already offers a variety of Advanced Driver Assist Systems across its entire range. Like Volvo it has also declared a vision of 'zero accidents'. Today's S-Class is already effectively a Level Three self-driving vehicle (the requirement that you maintain your hands on the steering wheel has more to do with insurance policies than with technological uncertainty). Zetsche has also noted: "For us, autonomous vehicles are an important step on the way to accident-free driving." Mercedes-Benz's commitment especially extends to trucks; at the 2014 International Commercial Vehicles Show in Hannover the Stuttgart giant presented its vision 'Future Truck 2025' and stated (conservatively) that in ten years its trucks will be able to drive autonomously on the motorways and highways of Europe.

- BMW has also confidently embraced certain autonomous features, with Werner Huber, its Head of Driver Assistance and Perception, describing in-house efforts as "the king-class of driver-assistance systems." True to form the company even released a deeply impressive video of a drifting 2-Series Coupe on YouTube and announced a collaboration with Baidu (China's Google) to launch self-driving cars. Nevertheless, like Daimler, they are a bit more modest when it comes to Level Four autonomy. Ludwig Willisch, CEO of BMW North America, laid out the automaker's convictions (and brand restrictions) at the 2014 Detroit Auto Show. "We would not say that going from A to B automatically should be done by the car. It should be done by the driver. Otherwise the whole notion of being the 'Ultimate Driving Machine' would go away."

- Volkswagen is similarly reserved in public; behind-the-scenes, however, they have been supporters of self-driving technology since the late 1990s. Their Silicon Valley Electronics Research Laboratory cooperates with Stanford University, and in 2005 a fully-autonomous VW Touareg won the Grand Challenge race (sponsored by DARPA). In 2014, VW acquired Blackberry's European research unit with an aim to focus it on Connected-Car technology; it also is leading a consortium of 29 firms and universities in a three-and-a-half year Automated Driving Applications & Technologies (AdaptIVe) project (funded by the EU) aimed at defining standards for Level 3 and 4 automation, as well as V2V communication.

- Honda, which already offers lane departure warning, adaptive cruise control and forward collision warning on most of its vehicles, had initially been caught out by the bullishness of its competitors. In August 2014, however, Jim Keller, Senior Manager of R&D for Honda in the Americas, suggested that 2020 would be a reasonable date for Honda. Barely one month later Honda showed off a fully autonomous Acura RLX prototype able to accelerate, brake, signal to change lanes and merge onto freeways. It also featured a V2V-supported 'virtual tow' system by which one vehicle provides guidance for followers.

- Toyota has publicly been oddly contrarian. Ken Koibuchio, General Manager of Intelligent Vehicle Development, said: "Driving is essentially very fun. Rather than making it seem like the driver can simply take a nap while sitting at the wheel, we need drivers to understand that there will be task-sharing involved." Nevertheless, several test-vehicle sightings give insight into what will be called Automated Highway Driving Assist, which includes lane trace control and adaptive cruise control. Both are (uniquely) supported by GPS and V2V communications.

- Unlike its aggressive entry into electric vehicles, General Motors lacked conviction with autonomous vehicles until mid-2014. "It'll happen, but it's a long way out," John Capp, the company's Director of Electrical, Controls and Active Safety Research, told the *New Yorker's* Burkhard Bilger. Unsurprising and perhaps correlated is that many analysts were reserved about the long-term stock performance of the company. To some surprise, in September 2014 GM's new CEO Mary Barra announced that an "all but fully autonomous" Cadillac CTS sedan, including certain V2V technologies, would be available with the 2017 model year. GM's Chief Technology Officer Jon Lauckner confronted naysayers and those eager for a one hundred percent solution head-on by adding: "We're not going to wait until we perfect a driverless system."

When Will You Be Able to Buy a Driverless Car

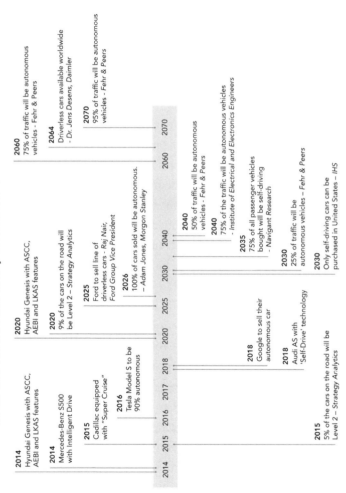

2014
Hyundai Genesis with ASCC, AEBI and LKAS features

2014
Mercedes-Benz S500 with Intelligent Drive

2015
Cadillac equipped with "Super Cruise"

2016
Tesla Model S to be 90% autonomous

2020
Hyundai Genesis with ASCC, AEBI and LKAS features

2020
9% of the cars on the road will be Level 2 – Strategy Analytics

2025
Ford to sell line of driverless cars - Raj Nair, Ford Group Vice President

2026
100% of cars sold will be autonomous. – Adam Jones, Morgan Stanley

2060
75% of traffic will be autonomous vehicles - Fehr & Peers

2064
Driverless cars available worldwide - Dr. Jens Desens, Daimler

2070
95% of traffic will be autonomous vehicles - Fehr & Peers

2018
Google to sell their autonomous car

2018
Audi A5 with 'Self-Drive' technology

2015
5% of the cars on the road will be Level 2 – Strategy Analytics

2040
50% of traffic will be autonomous vehicles – Fehr & Peers

2040
75% of the traffic will be autonomous vehicles - Institute of Electrical and Electronics Engineers

2035
75% of all passenger vehicles bought will be self-driving - Navigant Research

2030
25% of traffic will be autonomous vehicles – Fehr & Peers

2030
Only self-driving cars can be purchased in United States – IHS

2014 2015 2016 2017 2018 2020 2025 2030 2040 2060 2070

Sources: Mercedes-Benz, GM News, Strategy Analytics, Automotive News, Nissan News, Navigant Research, Volvo News, Fehr & Peers, Lux Research, IHS

- Ford, Google, Cadillac, Tesla and others have also been more or less bullish on their public predictions, summarized neatly by Mojomotors (page 99).

Supporting the major manufacturers is a slew of first- and second-tier suppliers. Bosch, who produces not just sparkplugs but also ultrasound, radio and video sensors, are shifting strategy to capture the potential of autonomous driving. They expect to produce over fifty million ultrasound sensors in 2015 – an essential requirement for the future of mobility. Bosch – who has also partnered with satellite navigation provider TomTom – expects to generate one billion euros from driver assistance systems by 2016, driving the path toward enabling high speed automated driving at least on the freeways by 2020.

With increased competition and economies of scale the cost of the technology is spiralling downward at a dizzying rate. The cost of lasers required for autonomous vehicles to 'see' around 360-degrees has fallen by ninety percent, from over $80,000 (c. €65,000 or £50,000) to less than $8,000, and is expected to drop to under $1,000 by 2018.

Importantly, the implementation of autonomous vehicle technologies based on existing road infrastructure – as it is being developed – does not depend on changing millions of miles of highway and urban streets. The Cato Institute notes in its September 2014 report *Policy Implications of Autonomous Vehicles*: "Organizations developing autonomous vehicles have presumed that smart infrastructure will not be available and instead designed their cars to operate using the existing infrastructure. This means that highly- and fully-autonomous vehicles must be very adaptable, as traffic signals, signs, and even roadway striping vary greatly from state to state."

Economic Benefits of Implementing the Technology

We have discussed the many benefits that come with switching from manual, semi-automatic vehicles to fully self-driving vehicles in this chapter. Let's now look at some other gains to be made.

Beyond 'zero accidents' one of the greatest benefits of progressing toward an autonomous transport system is the personal and collective reduction in (lost) driving time that comes as a result of not navigating roads for hours on end every day. This applies to both individual drivers and to professional drivers – in other words taxi drivers, freight-forwarders and drivers of public transportation.

In fact, the benefit, and therefore the impetus for implementing autonomous vehicle technology may be greatest in heavy commercial vehicle fleets, where decisions are made rationally with an eye to cost-effectiveness as well as minimizing driver time. That these vehicles are speed and lane limited, generally travel on highways and have predictable routing makes the truck industry a viable target for autonomy. According to the Rocky Mountain Institute (a not-for-profit think tank on ecological business models), autonomous vehicle technology will allow for drafting (vehicles travelling very close to each other to stay within an aerodynamic slipstream) that could result in fuel economy gains of twenty to thirty percent. Hence whichever logistics company is the first to take the driver away from the wheel, reduce the space between vehicles and cut out accidents in freight forwarding will see their value proposition (and profit) rise exponentially.

So, the self-driving vehicle could also take the role of professional drivers out of the picture. Economically, how is this beneficial? How can eliminating the jobs of close to 300,000 taxi and hackney-carriage drivers in the UK (and interestingly only a similar number in the US) be a benefit to society? It has to do, once again, with externalities and economics. Taxi drivers in the UK must study for years to acquire 'The Knowledge' at huge cost to themselves and their environment. In the US the licence to operate a taxi (signified by a medallion) can cost upward of $1 million in cities like New York. Both The Knowledge and the medallion are entirely artificial hurdles of entry, outdated and superseded by technology like satellite navigation systems and smartphone apps. Justus Haucap, former chairman of the German commission on monopolies and Economics Professor at the University of Düsseldorf explained: "The rules in the taxi market are partially absurd. Why would you today test geography, when knowledge of how to operate a navigation system is sufficient." I would argue that getting The Knowledge today is the equivalent of aspiring to be a typewriter repairman in 1985. It might work for five more years, but really I believe it's a recipe for career disaster which even governments should take an interest in mitigating. It's also an issue where the self-driving and shared vehicles trends come together – more on that later.

We're not staring at a future with hundreds of thousands of unemployed drivers, however. Just as the Internet didn't put typists and paper-producers out of business (in fact, the production of office paper initially increased upon the introduction of e-mail), the liberation of mind-power required to acquire The Knowledge. Taxi drivers are smart people who are currently roped into wasting time and money on outdated systems. Let's free them of this mandate and allow them to innovate customer-service on their own. Will we miss the irreverent banter? Perhaps, but collectively we should be glad that their skills and money will be applied in different sectors of the economy.

Another benefit to society is that self-driving vehicles will allow those who cannot drive, and especially the visually impaired or other physical disabilities, to travel from one destination to another effortlessly – including to work. This means that sight-impaired people, who without help might today be restricted to certain travel paths, may become more productive and innovate for society's benefit. As research has shown, other senses often compensate for failings in vision – Ray Charles and Stevie Wonder are good examples, and according to one study the blind have improved memory. Companies such as Punto Vision, Allianz Brazil, and UPP in Moscow have leveraged the combination of keen hearing and good memories by employing (with significant success) thousands of visually-impaired people. In the near future millions more will be enabled to get to a place of employment by way of autonomous vehicles.

Similarly, older people (think of your parents in the south of France, Mallorca, Florida, or Thailand) will be able to engage in more geographically diverse commercial and social pursuits. Rather than become greeters at the local Walmart – because it's the easiest position to get to – they can choose more productive pursuits away from home.

Overall autonomous vehicles will also improve the efficiency of transport systems and infrastructure, vastly improving punctuality and increasing road capacity while reducing congestion. Self-driving cars also eliminate the time-consuming and economically useless act of parking, while the costs of monitoring traffic will also tumble. An immense budgetary change will have to be made where city and municipal governments depend on parking fees and traffic fines for chunks of their revenue.

Cars without drivers will eventually reduce annual accident and death rates to close to zero; they will also almost expunge insurance costs, saving us all billions in insurance premiums. As I've said before, many insurance companies – as they currently exist – will be toast.

Many more industries will feel an economic impact from autonomous vehicle proliferation, and in a variety of ways – we'll explore some of them in the final chapter of this book. The reach extends well beyond the obvious ones however. Erin Griffith asked in the August 15th 2014 issue of *Fortune* magazine: "If driverless cars save lives, where will we get organs?" Bre Pettis, founder and CEO of the 3D printing company Makerbot noted: "We have this huge problem that we sort of don't talk about, that people die all the time from car accidents. It's kind of insane. But the most interesting thing is, if we can reduce accidents and deaths, then we actually have a whole other problem on our hands of, 'Where do we get organs?' I don't think we'll actually be printing organs until we solve the self-driving car issue. The next problem will be organ replacement." As is often the case, a problem raised by one industry's transformation will beget an opening for the adoption of new technologies in other industries. Fortunately, in this instance, researchers at Cornell University and others have already shown the promise of 3D printing organs.

Impact on Productivity

In its annual scorecard of traffic congestion, INRIX has found that Londoners lose on average eighty-one hours each year in traffic jams – excluding 'normal' commute times. This equates to nine working days (almost five percent of total work time) stuck behind the wheel. Belgium has the dubious honour of leading the national statistics for Europe with – on average, per citizen – a wincing fifty-nine hours wasted.

This time could be spent engaging in constructive pursuits instead of the monotony of our roads. INRIX is also convinced: "Future roads will not be built with concrete as much as they'll be built with software."

American drivers experience the same scenario. According to a study by Texas A&M University in 2011, *solely* traffic jams and congestion caused Americans to travel for an *extra* 5.5 billion hours. This also caused fuel purchases to increase by 2.9 billion gallons – a net retail impact of over $10 billion. Not surprisingly, the inactivity has increased carbon dioxide emissions by fifty-six billion pounds, and according to the same source the cost of the wasted time and fuel comes to a staggering $121 billion annually – $818 per driver. The need for autonomous vehicles therefore goes well beyond safety; it's an efficiency, environmental and economic 'no-brainer'.

On a local scale, Washington DC is by far the most congested city in America, with every driver confined in traffic for sixty-seven hours annually. That frightening figures means that people often have to spare an hour for a trip that would take twenty minutes in lighter traffic.

The total population of the US was 232 million in 1982. It has since increased by thirty-four percent to 312 million. The number of cars on the road was 122 million in 1980, more than doubling to 256 million by 2008 (since when the increase has thankfully plateaued). With that in mind, INRIX also suggested: "As GDP [of countries] goes up, average mph goes down." Wealthier countries have more traffic congestion. So, once again, the question that arises: Are cars making us more productive or less so, and can autonomous driving be the solution, helping us utilize time in a much more productive manner?

A Technology that Mimics Human Senses

There have been many (typically shallow and uninformed) debates centred on the pros and cons of autonomous vehicles controlling mobility around the world. Although people realize that 400-ton airliners have been cruising 'on autopilot' for years, that knowledge does little to eliminate the apprehensions on entering a car without a driver. However, experts who understand how safe and accident-proof a driverless vehicle is have other questions on their mind that have nothing to do with personal safety. In any case, in order to completely accident-proof our cities it's essential that the entire transport system be integrated, with road data sent vehicle-to-vehicle in real time.

An exclusively autonomous system working in conjunction with V2V communication, for instance, would see cars reacting according to potential hazards before sensors could even detect them as each vehicle communicates incidents to the 'swarm' of vehicles behind it. However, until the entire transport network shifts to an autonomous mode of travelling, accidents cannot be fully eliminated.

There are also still real technical hurdles to overcome. Even Chris Urmson, director of the Google car team and perhaps one of the most visible and notable proponents of autonomous vehicles, notes the limitations of his product. Currently driverless vehicles have a relative inability to navigate in certain urban environment; they can't detect potholes or spot uncovered manholes. They continue to have difficulties in environments where traffic lights might not be working, too, and where circulars (roundabouts) shrink momentarily to one lane, then back to three and where stop signs are occasionally stolen or fall down, where right before left (or vice versa) is dependent on driver communication or where police officers direct traffic against the usual flow or rules. These are all surmountable, however. Urmson told the *MIT Technology Review* in August 2014 that he wants the cars ready by the time his eleven-year old son is of legal driving age (sixteen in

California), giving him a deadline of 2019 – not unrealistic given Google's ability to gather, generate, process and deliver results on data.

This means that two key issues need to be addressed by then

- mobility in an unregulated environment
- mobility in a hybrid environment (there will be a long period of hybrid driving, which here means transportation networks that include both driven and self-driving cars).

Real benefits will come when our cars not only rely on their own sensing equipment but also use 'swarm intelligence' by collating data from vehicles around them. For example, if a vehicle 'learns' that another vehicle five car-lengths ahead just applied the brakes heavily it will know to prepare to do the same. In the same way we rely on the community-generated knowledge of Yelp and TripAdvisor to avoid bad hotels, adjusting our travel choices accordingly, vehicles will rely on communication from other cars that have been held up in congestion to avoid traffic jams and collisions more effectively, or to simply deduce the best route to the destination.

The members of the automotive industry are, each in their own way, developing sensors in order to provide solutions for the most common causes of human errors. These solutions include ensuring safety on high-speed routes as well as avoidance of congested routes. The systems are commonly known as Advanced Driver Assist Systems and they use sensors in combination with other tools such as cameras, radar, control units and actuators that knit together large quantities of data, allowing the vehicle to quickly make the best possible decision. Many of these solutions are already operational, while others are still in the planning phase. Either way, they will allow a vehicle to not only monitor but also communicate with its surroundings.

Sensor-based solutions for driver assistance use algorithms as well as cameras and radar to create a comprehensive three-dimensional picture of surroundings that can be monitored at speed. So far, although this artificial intelligence can understand what is directly in front of it, it cannot yet deduce the consequences of a specific act. For this rather thought-provoking development to take place the ability to mimic human processes and use historical knowledge to link events is required.

The limitation of such a technology resides chiefly in the cost of developing it, but also in the data points necessary to generate this 'fuzzy' logic, but neither of these represents an insurmountable hurdle (as Google has shown us with StreetView). Will consumers be willing to pay up to facilitate breakthroughs during the early stages until a more cost-effective technology is developed? The lidar system that Google's car is equipped with is not only complex but also expensive, initially costing roughly $70,000 per vehicle. As usual, however, the price of technology is falling rapidly. Start-up company Cruise Automation (founded by serial entrepreneur Kyle Vogt) began offering an add-on kit for Audi A4s in 2013 for $10,000. While the equipment doesn't offer full Level Four automation it does include cameras, sensors and radar that links into the car's cruise control, brakes, steering and engine management. The impressive result is a retrofit Level Three automation solution that in due course could be retrofitted in most modern vehicles.

On top of a sensor-based system, a Level Four self-driving car also needs to have full connectivity in order to bond with other vehicles on the road as well as with surrounding infrastructure. One of the most diligently tested technologies for this is DSRC – Dedicated Short-Range Communication – which uses radio waves.

In order to spread autonomous driving technology to every vehicle on the road certain policies encouraging widespread adoption need to be applied. These policies should encompass rules for scenarios where one or more of the car's sensors is obstructed and cannot function properly. In such a situation a car would require alternative technology allowing it to gather data and make decisions on its own. In a worst-case scenario, where the car loses its connection to the network and is consequently unable to communicate with other vehicles, it will need to have a backup plan – especially so if it no longer has a steering wheel and pedals.

Testing and Investing

At the University of Michigan a 'Mobility Transformation Center' will effectively simulate a city and highway within thirty-two acres of land, allowing researchers to test automated vehicle technologies with impunity. This will be an exceptional venture for the University – no other institute in the world has a comparable facility.

The so-called 'Mcity' will mimic the traffic of a city – even simulating dangerous traffic situations and road conditions in order to explore the limitations of a new technology.

With merged lanes as well as roundabouts, signs, stoplights, intersections and everything else that makes up a real road, the Mcity will include obstructions in the form of construction sites, school areas and – yes – robotic pedestrians. It will be a model of what the next generation of connected mobility will be like. The engineers at the University of Michigan will initially test a Ford Fusion Hybrid; collaboration with Ford will ensue to develop sensors for the car along with new mapping technology. Because the entire facility will be coded the engineers can change the traffic conditions to test any feature of a vehicle. For example, they can make a robotic pedestrian run in front of the car to see how the car would respond. Completion in Ann Arbor is scheduled for 2021 (notably *after* the first crop of autonomous vehicles are to have been released to the public).

In effect, these testing facilities are enabling the robotic artificial intelligence that allows vhicles to take full, proactive control, rather than be silent observers. While Mcity currently has the lead in ambition and implementation of testing facilities, there are now initiatives underway in the Silicon Valley (bearing in mind the presence and needs of Apple, Google and Tesla), South Carolina and Zurich.

Forbes estimates that the near-term market for autonomous vehicle technology is worth over $2 trillion in the US alone, and will be dominated not by hardware but by software solutions.

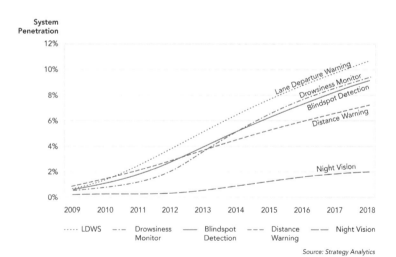

Source: Strategy Analytics

Legal Limitations

So, just as Asimov's prediction for autonomous vehicles (which will come sooner than the predicted 2057) has been revived, much is now being made of Isaac Asimov's three rules of robotics. In principle, any robot simply performs a series of tasks, as programmed by an engineer. Given a choice, the robot will also perform as per a series of programmed priorities.

Asimov's Rules of Robotics, 1942

1. *A robot may not injure a human being or, through inaction, allow a human being to come to harm.*
2. *A robot must obey the orders given to it by human beings, except where such orders would conflict with the First Law.*
3. *A robot must protect its own existence as long as such protection does not conflict with the First or Second Law.*

But is the work of a mid-twentieth century science-fiction writer even relevant for questions of liability and damage limitation that will be posed with self-driving cars? The question arises – and the time will come – when an autonomous car will need to choose between injuring its occupant and injuring a pedestrian. It's a gloomy decision made every day by drivers; perhaps as they skid along an icy road toward a storefront or as they look up from texting on a smartphone, only to discover they are hurtling toward a child in the street at irreversible speed.

Who will be liable for injuries and death?

With a driver onboard, the answer is clear – the (mobile phone using, texting, eating, or sleeping) individual behind the console of an autonomous vehicle will be considered a *licensed operator*, with which comes the responsibility to choose appropriately. No manufacturer can be held liable for the actions of the user, just as Apple wouldn't be responsible if instructions on how to make a bomb were written on an iPad.

Things get fuzzier as soon as any contribution to the process can be appointed and prevented, however, which in legal terms ventures into contributory negligence. If, say, bomb instructions were sold via eBay to hostile countries, perhaps eBay could be made partially liable, as this was a preventable use of its technology. Similarly, by way of negligence laws manufacturers have been made liable in many instances contributing to death – both rightfully (the Corvair, the Explorer, the Pinto and GM's most recent case of knowingly equipping cars with faulty ignition switches come to mind) and in cases of misapplication of the technology (the Audi 5000 and Toyota's unintentional acceleration cases, where drivers either confused brake and accelerator pedals or let their floor-mats get lodged in such a way that braking was inhibited). In the same way it's conceivable that negligent software or hardware design *could* be made liable for accidents or death. MSN has therefore rightly asked: "Will lawsuits kill the autonomous car?"

Likely not, as the key technology that makes an autonomous vehicle safe will also protect it from legal judgments. Autonomous vehicles keep reams of data on every turn, stop and go phase. That will make most scenarios crystal-clear. Or, as Sebastian Thrun puts it: "The big losers are going to be the trial lawyers."

Lloyd's of London (the world's marketplace for tricky insurance scenarios) has studied the insurance implications of an autonomous vehicle rollout in considerable detail. In an impressive report *Autonomous Vehicles: Handing Over Control: Risks and Opportunities in Insurance* (March 2014) it outlines the status quo: "In the UK at least, primary liability rests with the user of the car, regardless of whether their actions cause the accident or not. If defective technology caused the accident, the user (or their insurer) has to pursue this legally with the manufacturer. In addition, at present drivers are expected to maintain awareness and supervision of their car."

The report goes on to assess the future, when (notably, not 'if') "drivers become more like systems supervisors". It speculates prospects for motor insurance; while the need (and cost) for motor-liability insurance will be minimized, "some element of risk would be retained by the owner of a car. Damage or theft can still occur when a car is parked in a driveway… It is possible that this risk could become part of household contents policy coverage."

For the time being, governments (perhaps nudged a little themselves by the insurance and auto industry lobbies) are reluctant to change laws to transfer liability from the driver to manufacturers or (unlicensed) operators of autonomous cars. In all likelihood, however, licensing laws will be adapted so that passengers – as the Lloyd's report hints – become 'operators'. California's regulations on autonomous vehicles, announced in June 2014, do this by introducing a new class of licence.

The day will come, however, when a driverless vehicle kills a human being by way of an unavoidable accident, software flaw, virus, or even cyber fraud. *The New York Times* noted the following in May 2014:

- "The first deadly accident could be a bigger headache for the carmaker's public relations department than for its lawyers."
- "'It's the one headline, 'machine kills child,' rather than the 30,000 obituaries we have every year from humans killed on the roads,' said Bryant Walker Smith, a fellow at Stanford

University's Center for Automotive Research."

While this outcome will provoke endless discussion – and slow progress for a little while – it will be important for us to remember what will have been achieved by that point. Just like airbags have sadly killed people, they have saved many more.

Chapter 4:

Zero Ownership

" Are we paying too high a price for maintaining units of individual mobility (cars)? **"**

Is Ownership Foolish?

Traditionally products are bought in return for complete ownership. However, in recent years financing, flexible-duration leasing and sharing arrangements are making it possible to rent (or share, peer-to-peer) almost anything and use it for any duration based on terms decided between owner and user. This is known as the sharing economy (or to legal scholars the 'temporary access to rights') and the concept is becoming increasingly common.

The sharing economy is effectively an extension of the principles of collaborative content sharing (BearShare, KaZaa, Wikipedia, Wikimedia, YouTube, Khan Academy etc.) into the realm of consumption. Based on trust, a set of rules, scheduling and rating systems for users, it's now possible to find collaborative consumption models for anything from yachts and private planes (Smart Yacht, Social Flight and Fly Victor, to name but a handful) to vacation homes (Airbnb, HouseTrip and Couch Surfing), luxury fashion goods (Refashioner and Bag Borrow) and even municipal governments. Muni Rent, formed in southern Michigan in the summer of 2014, allows municipalities to share street sweepers, dump trucks and pavement rollers rather than purchasing them outright. In San Francisco there are more Airbnb homes available than big-chain hotel rooms, leaving a noticeable dent in revenues for traditional operators. As reported in a 2014 study by hotel industry consultancy HVS: "The rapidly expanding room count offered through Airbnb is on a trajectory to surpass that of the world's largest hotel chains, including InterContinental Hotels Group and Hilton Worldwide." Airbnb's CEO has tweeted triumphantly: "Marriott wants to add 30,000 hotel rooms [in 2014]. We will add that in the next two weeks."

According to *Forbes*, £2.2 billion ($3.5 billion) of revenue has already been generated by the collaborative-use economy for a range of products and services. This includes not only Airbnb's forty million total guests since 2007 but also a vast array of large- and small-scale enterprises, such as shared-use driveways for cars, pet baths, activity centres, or power tools (according to the *New York Times* there are eighty million power drills in the US today, each used on average thirteen minutes per year).

The modern sharing economy is built around the ancient concept of bartering within a community and, according to Airbnb founder Brian Chesky, trust: "Our core invention at Airbnb was probably our reputation system, which establishes trust between people. It gives people freedom to produce and make a living the way a company would." The organization has developed a flexible platform that allows people to offer room and board for rent – a major boon for anyone searching for short-term accommodation based on a mutually beneficial agreement.

So, is it still sensible for a household's greatest financial outlay outside of mortgages or rent to be on something used for only a few hours a day (or for an increasing number of urbanites just a few hours every month)? For many people, driving (and hunting for parking) is detrimental to their quality of life as well as their productivity. The questions raised are simple yet profound for many families: Are we paying too high a price for maintaining units of individual mobility (cars)? Given the many alternatives, is ownership still prudent?

Car-sharing Models

A sharing economy for vehicles works in two distinct ways (which serves to confuse the term a bit): car-sharing *with* and *without* third-party drivers (and I'll call them third-party drivers, as these people are not always professionals). We'll expand on each of these a bit later.

Car-sharing *with* third-party drivers is an amalgamation of taxis (or hackney carriages, as they've existed for over 300 years in London) and carpooling. Subscribers offer their cars and passenger seats to services such as Lyft and Uber with the aim of generating additional income. The model works something like this:

You want a ride to destination B. After installing the app of a car-sharing service you enter your desired destination. Because your smartphone knows your location (A), within minutes you find yourself in a car driven from A to B by either the owner or an employee, depending on how the service works. Billing is usually carried out directly via the app (which has stored previously entered credit-card details).

With the trend of thinking out of the (hotel and taxi) box firmly established, the sharing economy provides a platform that permits us new and innovative ways to receive and offer a variety of products and services – and to earn money not controlled by the mercy of corporations. This is one of the many reasons why we're becoming increasingly comfortable with an economy that allows multiple avenues of participation, instead of working for a company. Brian Chesky said in an interview with the UK's *Sunday Telegraph*: "We used to live in a world where there were people and there were businesses. Now we live with a third category, which is people as businesses. What that's doing is bringing the world back to where it used to be... The world is going a little bit back to the village."

The Broader Ambitions of Uber et al.

Though the concept of *driven* ride-sharing is hardly new, it's gaining substantial traction through the launch of global business models evidenced by Uber, Hailo, Lyft, Get Taxi, Sidecar and China's Didi Dache – all essentially software companies providing a platform for independent taxi operators and companies. The consequence is a more accessible city, with drivers keen for increased business and more people searching for a convenient lift. These platforms can now be found in thousands of cities, with their continuously increasing services helping people connect in exchange for a small fee. Uber's ambitions are grander, however: according to its founders the company is "evolving and revolutionizing the world's transport system".

Uber's low-fare service is expanding globally, acquiring drivers to use their software wherever it goes and cutting prices every day. It's fare quotes are made irresistible in an effort to gain market share in particular against traditional cabs (as well as walking, cycling and public transport). The company has also capitalized on widespread smartphone ownership to turn booking into an anytime-anywhere process taking only seconds. Just as physically hailing a cab has been the status quo for generations, conjuring up a lift from an app-enabled car-sharing service is the new norm.

But what is the difference between a traditional taxi and car-sharing? After all, both carry out the same function.

The chief discrepancy is that car-sharing exists through unlicensed drivers (that could be anyone) sharing their cars on a short-term basis for either one or multiple riders and destinations. This creates a partial transfer of responsibility toward the user, who is responsible for partially dictating terms they are comfortable with as opposed to accepting terms imposed by a city's taxi cartel (much to the chagrin of those who are deeply invested in the cartels).

As more freelance drivers (and also future-minded driving professionals) join on these platforms, the concept of car-sharing will become more widely acceptable and utilized, despite a battle to uphold cartels (see *The Hopeless Battle Against Uber and Lyft*, below). Innovative models will continue to circumvent restrictions imposed by unions and city licensing services. Indeed, many standards are yet to be discovered – and potential realized – as constant innovation is evolving the mechanicals of the car-sharing business. Some companies are offering to set up a platform where suppliers and demanding customers can meet up and discuss their own terms to strike a deal, while others prefer receiving supplier and rider requests separately then organizing the system to make the best match in terms of car demands, affordability and routes.

The Hopeless Battle Against Uber and Lyft

In the summer of 2014 taxi drivers throughout Europe and the US attempted to stand their ground against the launch of Uber.

"Uber is a threat to our legal system. It ignores laws, undermines social conventions and creates a grey-market, from which only investors will profit," protested a German transport minister in North Rhine-Westphalia.

That these services don't have to follow the archaic laws governing most taxi and car-service companies caused heated debate, and Uber and its peers were even prevented from launching (temporarily) in cities all over the world: New York, Paris, all of Germany.

The driving force behind the bans was an exceptionally scared community of taxi cartels that convinced courts their licensing procedures have some sort of stabilizing element, with implications for the safety and comfort of riders. To add weight to their arguments taxi drivers in London, Berlin, Paris, Madrid, Chicago and Sao Paolo went on strike for a day. They felt (and still feel) that this new breed of personal mobility should be subject to the same withering set of policies and formalities that have defined their profession for generations.

It's a culture clash that's already causing lawmakers to overreact and draw up new laws to govern car-sharing services. How these laws manifest will be decisive in how the sharing economy pans out. If they restrict who and who is not allowed to participate in a sharing economy they could severely check all that is good about this emergent new system (although I truly don't believe this will happen). Taxi cartels will continue to test the flexibility of car-sharing systems, however, delaying the inevitable. The smarter communal governments and councils are keenly aware of the benefits of Uber et al., as the sharing economy also allows us to derive not just more rent from the economy, but more satisfaction. Many people are simply longing for a crowd-rated alternative to unfriendly cab drivers in threadbare vehicles with uncomfortable vinyl seats.

Any near-term 'victories' from strikes and temporary injunctions will be hollow. Moreover, the protests are having an additional effect. Pierre-Dimitri Gore-Coty, Uber's General Manager of Western and Northern Europe, told the Wall Street Journal: "It's going to make Uber even more visible, and make a lot of people realize that they now have choices that they didn't have before." Ironically, rather than causing transport chaos the taxi strike actually fuelled business for Uber and its competitors, in many cases alienating customers from the traditional black (or yellow) cabs completely. Both riders and drivers appear to be voting with their feet: the fact that there are now more Uber drivers than taxi drivers in cities like New York and London indicates that just perhaps some drivers are joining the future, rather than fighting against it.

Driving, but Not Owning

Cottoning-on to the trend of on-demand, pay-per-mile transportation and access-over-ownership, manufacturers and entrepreneurs have devised *self-driving* car-sharing concepts. Global membership of these models now numbers more than 3.5 million, according to Frost & Sullivan, and is expected to rise to twenty-five million by 2020.

Until recently the most successful globally-branded car-sharing model was early-mover Zipcar. Based on successful mobility cooperatives operating in Switzerland, Zipcar was founded in Boston in June 2000 by Antje Danielson and Robin Chase (who in 2009 was named one of *Time Magazine*'s one hundred most influential people). It quickly rolled out to

Washington, DC, New York and a number of college campuses throughout the US on the back of surprisingly little initial investment - $100,000 of outside funding and a leasing arrangement through General Electric. Now owned by Avis Budget, the company maintains its distinctive personality and is now available in over one-hundred US cities as well as in Austria, Canada, France, Spain, Turkey and the UK. The service boasts close to one million members.

The theory behind initiatives such as ZipCar is simple. Via computer or a smartphone app members can locate and reserve vehicles from a fleet consisting of primarily Volkswagens, Audis and BMWs (in Europe), or Toyotas, Hondas and Fords of various sizes (in the US). The cars are parked at dedicated on-street locations and in parking lots throughout participating cities. Arriving at the car, a membership card is swiped over an RFID reader in the window, opening the vehicle. With the keys in the glovebox members are then ready to go, to be charged on an hourly basis at a rate that includes fuel, insurance, inspection (MOT), taxes, road usage and congestion charging fees. Given the simplicity of the model and the availability of vehicles, most Zipcar users admit their transport habits have changed. Indeed, many will have given up on their second (or third) car. I, for one, have up to six Zipcars available to me at any given time within half a mile of my flat in London and have given up on owning even a first vehicle.

Depending on which city you're in, some car-sharing providers also allow for one-way, point-to-point driving (picking up the vehicle in one place and dropping it off elsewhere), which makes these models perfect 'last-mile' complements to public transportation.

Daimler and BMW (and some others) have started their own car-sharing companies, generally offering standardized vehicles. Daimler's fast-growing car2go provides Smart models in thirty European and North American cities with an aim to expanding to 50 cities by 2016. At the end of 2014 car2go counted one million members (a substantial increase from 600,000 in 2013), meaning it has now eclipsed ZipCar. Furthermore, Daimler's service is evolving to include 'car2go black', which will for the first time enable station-based two-way car-sharing using larger Mercedes-Benz B-Class vehicles. The scheme will give members the option of longer rental periods and targets a new kind of membership demographic, effectively competing for the weekend-getaway market with traditional rental companies and trains. Initially Hamburg and Berlin will receive one hundred cars each.

BMW's equivalent, DriveNow, was launched with some slick marketing in Munich in June 2011. By mid-2015 it had expanded to include ten cities (including San Francisco, Vienna, Seattle and London) and 300,000 customers – with an aim to expanding to 25 cities by 2020. Like Toyota's Ha:Mo pilot project in Toyota City, Japan, and Grenoble, France, DriveNow at least partially embraces the combination of zero emissions and zero ownership. It is using a fleet of hundreds of all-electric BMW i3 models in San Francisco and Copenhagen.

Combining both zero emissions and zero ownership on the basis of fuel-cell technology, start-up Microcab Industries of Coventry, UK, is a clear example of the future of mobility. Microcab's H2EV boasts a chassis engineered by Lotus and is unique to the service, like Bolloré's Bluecar. John Jostins, CEO and Founder of Microcab, described his plans to me:

> "We will be launching a 200 vehicle, community car club, which will replace around 2,000 privately owned vehicles, and emit zero carbon dioxide. Our fuel-cell

vehicles are specifically-designed for this purpose, and it will be based around a central location and can therefore make-do with a single hydrogen refilling station."

Of the American giants, Ford, via its Ford Motor Credit arm and in collaboration with Getaround, has most aggressively embraced car-sharing. In mid-2015, Ford launched a peer-to-peer sharing program to selected owners, allowing them to share the cost and use of their own vehicle. As CEO Mark Fields notes, "Customers, particularly in urban areas, want access, not ownership."

Upshift is a notable independent app-enabled service based in San Francisco that allows members to get a car for the day delivered straight to their door – eliminating even the minor hurdle of allocating a shared vehicle. Founder Ezra Goldman sees the potential for an integrated ecosystem of smartphone-enabled, on-demand mobility solutions. He created Upshift out of the need for a simpler day-trip option. His claim best summarizes the spirit of car-sharing: "Put down your keys. Pick up your smartphone. Your next car fits in your pocket. This is freedom."

Consequences for the Automobile Industry

Old school car-sharing – that is, carpooling to get from the suburbs to the city – has shown that passenger-less cars are a waste of space and energy. It has also taught carmakers that the end of single-occupancy vehicles (at least in urban areas) is nigh.

The next step is to increase the number of passengers and reduce countless hours of unused vehicular idle-time, thereby improving the overall flow of traffic through reduction in vehicle numbers. In other words: professionalizing carpooling (i.e. car-sharing).

Alix Partners revealed that car-sharing services are responsible for 500,000 vehicle non-sales during the past decade. They suggest that sales will suffer by a further 1.2 million cars by 2021. Similarly, in 2014 researchers at the Transportation Sustainability Research Center at the University of California, Berkley, estimated that one self-driven car-share vehicle replaced between six and twenty-three cars in the US and between four and ten cars in Europe. Is it any wonder that traditional carmakers such as BMW and Daimler are manoeuvring to secure a piece of this sector early?

IHS Automotive suggests that the rise in car-sharing and similar alternatives will lead to a levelling-off of global annual vehicle sales as early as 2020.

Extracting data from smartphones is making it easier to ascertain the location of a person seeking a car and develop new routes or corridors of high usage. That data can then be used to improve the efficiency of the entire network, ensuring people have a ride available within a few minutes of requesting it.

Zero Ownership and Auto Design

As awareness and availability of car-sharing grows, people are beginning to realize how futile it is to bind their capital in an asset with few justifiable returns. Depending on which city you're in, each shared vehicle replaces between ten and twelve that are privately-owned, leaving a dent in the balance sheets of manufacturers.

Today, European and American car manufacturers are still able to hide business lost to car-sharing initiatives

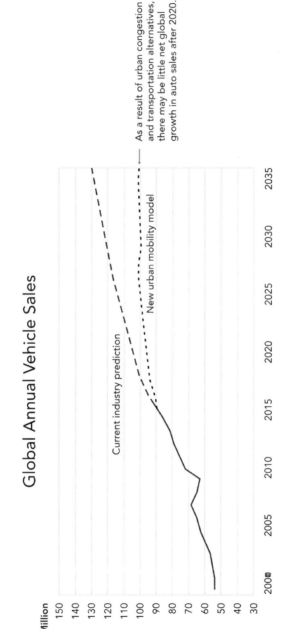

Global Annual Vehicle Sales

Current industry prediction

New urban mobility model

As a result of urban congestion and transportation alternatives, there may be little net global growth in auto sales after 2020.

Source: IHS Automotive

behind staggering growth rates in China and the Middle East. Moreover, car-sharing organizations still have to purchase standard-issue vehicles from manufacturers and dealers. As these organizations and their volume orders continue to grow, however, they will begin to flex their financial muscle, insisting on fleet-orders and even dedicated vehicle specifications and designs.

Remember when cars were purchased outright and a car's design only changed every seven or eight years? In the same way that leasing (and financing) has effectively replaced outright car ownership and ushered in three-year design lifecycles for new cars, building vehicles for shared ownership will rebalance design priorities for vehicles. While cars today have barely more than ten percent utilization rates (in terms of time), shared vehicles will have over fifty percent utilization rates (i.e. five times more mileage driven per year), significantly shifting the product design specification toward durability and utility. Expect traditional manufacturers to build cars specifically designed for the rigours of car-sharing in the future, in much the same way that London, New York and other cities have specifically-designed taxis, or that UPS is able to specify and order dedicated-build vehicles for its fleet of delivery vehicles. On the cover of this book, you can see one immensely talented designer's vision of a Three Zeroes vehicle. Similarly, the design company IDEO in November 2014 released a few of its own ideas via Wired magazine. The Mobility Revolution will spark a renaissance of creativity and boldness in the design of vehicles within (and outside of) the design studios of major manufacturers.

Taking it a step further, and away from the traditional manufacturers, Autolib' – a car-sharing network that started in Paris using electric vehicles –

operates around 3,000 of its own unique 'Bluecar' vehicles. Designed and engineered by Italy's Pininfarina, the Bolloré vehicles are built exclusively for the car-sharing company's requirements, using Bolloré's proprietary battery technology. After Paris and Indianapolis, Bolloré now has its sights set on London. Christophe Arnaud, Deputy Chief Marketing Officer for Blue Solutions (the division of Bolloré that launched Autolib' in Paris), told me the company is aiming for roughly 6,000 charging points and vehicles in the city, which will allow for effective short-distance, zero-emission car-sharing – all with its own uniquely designed vehicles.

As Daimler, BMW and the rest embark on in-house car-sharing schemes, and car-sharing providers enter into manufacturing, we will see the line between manufacturer and service provider gradually disappear. Furthermore, the sheer scale of these ambitions will continue to grow; China's Kandi, a NASDAQ listed manufacturer of go-karts and all-terrain vehicles, has started building its electric 'EV' exclusively for car-sharing in Huangzhou. It intends to have a fleet of 100,000 vehicles available from automotive vending machines available by 2016.

Which Model, Which Time?

With escalating technology, smartphones and the increasing availability of an Internet connection on the go, we have an array of tools that can be used to create platforms facilitating temporary access for a variety of options.

Given those options, how then to decide between chauffeured and user-driven car-sharing models (at least, until we are picked up by autonomous vehicles)? In a connected urbanized world, progressive meta-apps like Daimler's Moovel and Rome2Rio present us with the most integrated transport based on preferences, time and cost.

On a continuum, this might mean that

- walking and cycling in urban areas is undertaken where available, but replaced by Uber and Lyft for typically unintended shorter journeys. These services will take the place of taxis, or support the work of taxis in the case of Hailo and Gett.

- planned longer distances will be best undertaken on public transport, or alternatively via point-to-point car-sharing services like Autolib', BluePoint, DriveNow, or car2go. As BluePoint's Christophe Arnaud says: "We see [it] as a *complement* to public transport." Despite a theoretical driving range of 250 km the average rental time for Autolib' vehicles is less than thirty minutes. Similarly, for DriveNow and car2go in Germany it hovers between fifty and seventy-five minutes. In other words these vehicles are used for intra-city, point-to-point or return-to-base task mastering (a favourite, oft-cited example is the quick jaunt to IKEA or the home-improvement store). In urban areas where parking costs are exorbitant and congestion charges apply they may well even replace primary vehicles, and sooner rather than later.

- for trips of several hours, up to several days, user-driven (for now) car-sharing models like ZipCar and car2go will continue to serve the needs of drivers for the next five to ten years. Budget-minded long-range riders are also flocking to fast-growing BlaBlaCar, which offers its 20 million members in 18 countries to share their journey costs.

Security and Safety – Hurdles and Opportunity

Some argue that the sharing economy will give rise to safety issues. Risk, for instance, naturally increases when you get into a car with a driver you don't know. For this reason taxi drivers go through a lengthy process of identity confirmation among other safety measures. It means they are easy to trace, which of course makes it harder for them to commit a crime. If the same laws are applied to a new generation of mobility services they will restrict the flexible nature of a sharing economy. As a pseudo-preventative measure, services like Uber and Lyft have put various safeguards in place. However, not all services are the same. The key to success – evidenced by Airbnb – is the established trust vested in the community ratings model (although this is still a grey area).

In order to continue improving the car-sharing model (and make it more palatable to nervous skeptics) several things need to be perfected. Naturally, initiatives need to expand further, incorporating today's suburban areas. There are security issues to remedy, too, as well as improving the efficiency of the model, making it more cost-effective for users. Social limitations still exist to the community-trust model; some generations still hesitate getting into a car with a stranger, while others feel uncomfortable with online-only transactions. Perhaps there will continue to be a market for cash-only, suited, booted and licensed taxi-drivers – at least for a little while – to address these laggards. Google and others, however, understand that our current transport system is flawed and the imperative need for a better, more efficient system.

Beyond Uber's model, Google Ventures has invested in a number of alternate car-sharing schemes, such as RelayRides and Sidecar, which address various segments of the market (some of these use drivers who are explicitly licensed and presumably responsible). No doubt, the investments will go beyond this.

Whatever the model, the point for mobility is that instead of lugging around empty cars there is potential to generate income from filling seats and letting people ride along with you – whatever the destination. In the morning, a person headed to work can pick up passengers whose destination is close to his or her workplace and generate an income without any additional costs whatsoever. Monetizing and professionalizing carpooling makes the transport system more efficient and more attractive.

Burkhard Bilger's *New Yorker* article 'Inside Google's Driverless Car' summarizes Sergey Brin's real vision: "Most cars are used only for an hour or two a day. The rest of the time, they're parked on the street or in driveways and garages. But if cars could drive themselves, there would be no need for most people to own them. A fleet of vehicles could operate as a personalized public transportation system, picking people up and dropping them off independently, waiting at parking lots between calls. They'd be cheaper and more efficient than taxis – by some calculations they'd use half the fuel and a fifth the road space of ordinary cars – and far more flexible than buses or subways. Streets would clear, highways shrink and parking lots turn to parkland."

Will Zero Ownership Make Us a Closer-knit Society?

There is a broader impact beyond allowing non-owners access to affordable rides, one that is best exemplified by BlaBlaCar. With over 2 billion shared kilometers driven since its founding in 2004, the platform is not just creating efficiency in vehicle use (saving fuel and cost), but is effectively bringing communities closer together while allowing them to help each other. As ZipCar co-founder Robin Chase writes in her book, *Peers Inc.*, the overall economy is moving toward sharing – for financial and personal gain. Ultimately, this will aid economies because people will take greater advantage of resources available to them. Rides and vehicles aside, access to any number of infrequently-used assets will continue to revolutionize the consumer world, optimizing the use of our resources, and driving the sharing-economy further.

For centuries societies have drawn apart, with individuals focused on making it work for them. With a sharing economy on the rise people are taking time to learn more about others. The result is a society that collaborates and goes out of its way for the benefit of others, fostering flexibility and fiscal savings. This is also an economy that is moving toward betterment, albeit at a snail's pace. In the next twenty to thirty years, however, the impact of these changes will be keenly felt.

Chapter 5:

Outlook and Impact of the Three Zeroes

" Truly novel ideas require a clean sheet of paper; they must be unencumbered by the ball-and-chain of legacy production capacities, thinking and staff. **"**

By now it should be clear that we are at a tipping point in the evolution of the automobile industry – a point of no return where a combination of external factors will by 2020 have changed the automobile industry much more toward a 'mobility tool supplier' model. Those externalities are

- previously unknown and well-financed competitors
- rapidly changing consumer demographics and demand
- shifting governmental support (and incentives) away from traditional automakers and toward new and 'green' technologies and business models

It's also a perfect storm of internal factors, with

- the need to create multiple new business models straining resources
- shortening product cycles (from every eight years to yearly online updates)
- dwindling cash (through a combination of low interest rates, the need to 'shotgun' projects against new competitors,

and much more cautious investors)
- disillusioned staff (more eager to go to quickly-growing start-ups)

The above leave the traditional automotive industry in a similar position to the financial industry in 2000 (pre-9/11) and 2008 (pre-Lehman Brothers). Worse still is that in cases of transformation and upheaval the long-term view doesn't favour the incumbents.

Given the significance of the automobile industry in several large economies (Germany's automobile industry provides jobs to approximately fourteen percent of its employable citizens, constitutes twenty percent of total industrial R&D investment, and, rather worryingly, represents around forty-one percent of total automotive revenue for the entire EU), getting it right is not just a theoretical exercise – it's a national matter of depression or survival and growth.

The Automotive Industry: Losing the War for Talent

The risk of executive hubris and complacency will always loom large for those who can't see beyond incremental change. History proves that anyone who dares to dream big can find fame and success far greater than companies that prefer to play it safe. Those companies are not prepared to take the risks required to innovate, and then often regret not taking the initiative beforehand.

In truth, most players in the automotive industry have meanwhile become aware of what's in store for personal mobility and are either working on prototypes that mirror Tesla and Google's ambitions or acquiring companies that will stretch the boundaries of their current business model (note BMW, Daimler and Audi's joint purchase of Nokia's Here digital mapping division). This still leaves the incumbents one step behind, however. Truly novel ideas require a clean sheet of paper; they must be unencumbered by the ball-and-chain of legacy production capacities, thinking and staff.

With that in mind, public perception gives Google a decided edge in the race to full vehicle autonomy. One analyst has noted that to maintain its lead as an auto-industry outsider, Google just needs to continue doing what it does best – defying imagined rules and limitations and continuing to birth ideas that the world didn't believe were possible. At the very least they are redefining the automobile industry as an online-update software industry. More sweepingly, they are evolving ideas on how and where we work, live and move. As Mark Reuss, Product Development Chief at General Motors, said: "If they set their mind to it, I have no doubt [that Google could] become a very serious competitive threat." (Bloomberg, 28 May 2014.) According to KPMG, consumers are even more likely to buy a self-driving car from Google.

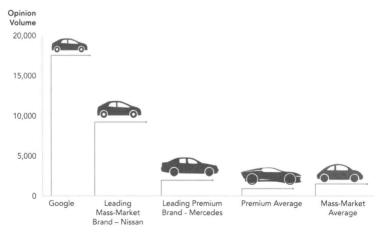

Source: KPMG MOBI™ Data

The public relations departments at some carmakers contend that Google is going out of its way to make the driverless concept seem easier and safer than it is. This is a natural, defensive reaction. The Technology and Innovation Policy Director of Toyota, Hilary Cain, said that one of the greatest barriers to self-driving car propagation will be uncertainty regarding future regulations. When we compare this to Uber and Google's 'shoot first, ask questions later' approach, we get an answer to why Toyota lags behind, at least with respect to the trend toward full vehicle autonomy. What's more, the digital native generation (raised on Facebook and perfect transparency of all their tweets and messages) is accustomed to working this way.

A new wave of disruptive, automotive entrepreneurialism, works differently to the 'analyse first and react' mentality of the past and stands to gain from studying the Industrial Revolution. One hundred years ago demand for saddle and horseshoe manufacturing dropped dramatically with the advent of the automobile. Today, automotive manufacturing is becoming as redundant as the horseshoe-maker. Demand for automotive engineers and assembly line staff will fall, as will the need for central production plants and complex logistics, even more so when cars can be 3D-printed (Phoenix-based Local Motors exhibited its first drivable 3D-printed vehicle in September 2014. It was printed in forty-four hours using $3,500-worth of material. Similarly, in August 2015, a battery-electric scooter named Paolo was released, designed to be 3D-printable, and with the potential to change the streetscape of most emerging economy cities).

Stian Westlake, Executive Director of Research at Nesta wrote in *City AM* (9 October 2014): "Most of the cars of the future will be highly durable workhorses for urban car-sharers, and software will represent a lot of their value." Though automotive manufacturers have been busy hiring coders and electrical engineers, some are still limited by location. Mechanical engineers and automotive craftsmen once thought nothing of making their homes and fortunes in the suburbs of Detroit, the UK's Midlands and Wolfsburg, but programmers prefer the action of a start-up to the stability of the status quo, and places like Silicon Valley, New York, Singapore and London.

Google, Tesla, Uber and Apple have successfully recruited hundreds of the best automotive designers from OEMs and the best robotics engineers from universities with a promise of being involved in changing the status quo. The threat to established companies is real and large, and it can't be addressed with engineers from headquarters in Detroit, Tokyo, Munich and Paris. The battle is being fought elsewhere, with a new breed of soldier.

Kodak, Smith Corona and The Innovator's Dilemma Within Automobile Companies

History is littered with fragments of companies that did not transform or evolve when faced with disruptive innovation. Two examples (both, notably, from my longtime home of Upstate New York) should serve as warnings to traditional car manufacturing in the US.

Despite inventing digital photography and building the first consumer digital camera in 1994 (the QuickTake, on behalf of Apple), Kodak doggedly clung to its old cash-cow film even as new technology took off.

The reason Kodak didn't build a successful strategy to meet fresh customer demand is because directors were so afraid of losing an existing and already successful business blueprint, according to George S. Day, Professor of Marketing at Wharton School of the University of

Pennsylvania and Co-director at Wharton's Mack Institute for Innovation Management.

Like Kodak, Smith Corona was a paradigm of success, market-domination and expansion for more than one hundred years. Founded in 1886, it grew to become a global leader in the typewriters, with a market share of over fifty percent and annual sales revenue greater than $500 million. The company scarcely recognized computers and word-processing as a danger. In November 1992, well after the launch of personal computers, CEO G. Lee Thompson said: "Many people believe that the typewriter and word-processor business is a buggy-whip industry, which is far from true. There is still a strong market for our products in the United States and the world." When asked what new products and services the company planned to introduce, he replied: "Nothing right now. They're still in the formative stages." True to form, Smith Corona lethargically confronted the word-processing transformation with a subtle evolutionary approach – it added screens to its typewriters and created a short-lived market for 'personal word processors'.

But what does this mean for the auto industry? You can't possibly compare typewriters to cars… can you? Well, yes, you can.

Traditional automobile manufacturers have – perhaps buried deep within their structures – actually known for decades that the future of automotive doesn't feature a combustion engine, yet the impetus, ability and desire to change has been limited. While they may have the resources, technology and moral imperative to change, they also have an economic and social responsibility to their shareholders, employees and communities to continue on a path of evolution, pushing ahead (and downplaying) the inevitable transformation but maximizing profits in the here and now. One senior executive at a German manufacturer told me: "We know we need to embrace the future, but we also need to take our responsibility to our employees seriously – we have tens of thousands of traditionally-educated staff, which we need to take along for the ride. They are skeptical of electric, they certainly don't buy into autonomous and they are scared of car-sharing. Convincing them takes time."

As outlined in Clayton Christensen's monumental work, The Innovator's Dilemma: When New Technologies Cause Great Firms to Fail, traditional companies are often hemmed in by their own structures and the opportunity-cost of developing an unknown proposition against evolving their successful current models. The internal structures of these companies are built around continual improvement at component level; they thus fail to leverage potential changes in their entire architecture and open the space for new players.

Part of the blame also lies at the feet of marketing strategy departments, whose relentless desire to protect their product planning through self-serving, often poorly worded market research leads to whitewashed evolution rather than true revolution. Henry Ford is reputed to have said (although there is some senseless debate on the matter): "If I had asked people what they wanted, they would have said faster horses." IDEO's Tom Kelly puts it a bit more bluntly: "Don't expect customers to help you envision the future."

So what is the solution? Christensen followed up his initial work in The Innovator's Solution: Creating and Sustaining Successful Growth, where he suggests that: "Identifying disruptive footholds means connecting with specific jobs that people – your future customers – are trying to get done in their lives." This isn't a contradiction, but a nuance for strategists. To truly innovate, it's necessary to watch and learn from your customers and gain an understanding of their problems or inherent needs, not to simply ask them what they want.

Christensen notes that disruptive technologies typically enable new markets to emerge. Evidencing this is Tesla, achieving what GM couldn't in the 1990s by creating an electric vehicle with market demand, sociopolitical support and an infrastructure to overcome the largest hurdle to electric vehicles: range-anxiety.

In the US, Scott Belcher, president of the nonprofit Intelligent Transportation Society, strongly believes in this contemporary age of disruption. He told New York Times in October 2014: "We're at the cusp now of this completely new generation of transportation, and it's going to change things on a scale not seen since Eisenhower and the Interstate Highway System."

(It's worth noting that it was the Interstate system that gave rise to the suburbs in the US in the 1970s and 1980s.)

On the subject of 'where' the battle is being fought, we shouldn't forget the world's dominant superpower-in-waiting. According to an analysis by research firm Lux, the US and Europe are initially expected to lead the market for self-driving cars. China, however, will soon grow to capture at least thirty-five percent market-share by 2030. Lux also predicts that the main factor responsible for the growth will be software.

BYD, Tesla and the Threat Beyond Automotive

On its website Chinese carmaker BYD describes itself as a top high-tech enterprise in China specializing in 'IT, Automotive and New Energy'. A 200,000-employee-strong company with the largest order book of rechargeable batteries in the world, it is a one of a number of new companies and brands that represent a significant threat to incumbent automotive giants. While some in Detroit scoff – and the majority of people will never have heard of BYD – the Sage of Omaha, Warren Buffett, invested $230 million for a ten percent stake in BYD in 2008 and in April 2014 Daimler revealed the first model of a joint-venture in the form of an all-electric vehicle brand: Denza. In 2013 and 2014, BYD was the best selling domestic Chinese brand (both for electric and conventional vehicles) and in 2014 generated $70 million in profit. Perhaps even more significantly, BYD has amassed an order volume of 4,000 all-electric *buses*, and also launched the world's largest electric vehicle – a 120-person electric bus with an operating range of 270 km (170 miles). Furthermore, its electric e6 crossover vehicle is just beginning to roll out worldwide. So watch this space: while BYD's first electric car is neither particularly attractive nor a performance champion, it has a significant range of 186 miles, and has become a favourite among taxi companies and fleet operators. For BYD producing vehicles is not even the end unto itself – it just happens to be an excellent showcase for its batteries.

Infinitely more recognizable in the West than BYD or Qoros, Tesla stormed into the automobile market and has since been accepted as a serious threat – and not just to the automotive industry. A collection of quotes from Elon Musk illustrates the passion and ambitions of the man who runs Tesla and Space X, is invested in SolarCity and dreamt up the 'Hyperloop'.

• "I don't think people quite appreciate the gravity of what is going on [with regard to global warming] or just how much inertia the climate has. We really need to do something."
• "Until every car on the road is electric, we will not stop."

- From a 2006 blog entry titled *The Secret Tesla Motors Master Plan*: "The overarching purpose of Tesla Motors (and the reason I am funding the company) is to help expedite the move from a mine-and-burn hydrocarbon economy toward a solar electric economy, which I believe to be the primary, but not exclusive, sustainable solution."
- "We should be able to do ninety percent of miles driven [autonomously] within three years." (told to the *Financial Times* in 2014, just a few *months* before releasing an updated Tesla Model S with semi-autonomous features to match the trend-setting Mercedes-Benz S-Class.)

The courage and scale of his ambitions are what drives fear into the boardrooms of not only the automobile industry. Morgan Stanley's automotive analyst Adam Jones (perhaps a slightly biased source, considering his employer has underwritten each of Tesla's share offerings) gushes about Elon Musk's company: "Tesla's quest to disrupt a trillion-dollar car industry offers an adjacent opportunity to disrupt a trillion-dollar electric utility industry. If it can be a leader in commercializing battery packs, investors may never look at Tesla the same way again." So Tesla isn't merely a threat to traditional automakers and public transport companies, but to energy providers, too, given its historic $5 billion investment in energy storage (i.e. batteries) at its Gigafactory. Why? Because storing energy is not relevant to personal transport alone. It is central to nearly every conceivable human activity, from production to living to shopping – in everything we do we are confronted with a need for energy. In April 2015, Tesla launched its Powerwall personal energy storage units, highlighting the company's desire and ability to not just produce batteries for cars but also for living (on Earth, or Mars – your choice, says Musk). "They will be for anyone who wants to buy them, really," the South Africa-born entrepreneur says of the Gigafactory-built stationary battery packs. "There will be quasi-infinite demand for battery storage if the energy density and the price are good enough."

Energy companies currently exist and operate on the principle of maximum-load (peak use) one-way supply. For most people, generating energy (beyond perhaps their own solar-powered micro-stations) is 'out of scope', as their peak usage time (night-time) doesn't coincide with their peak generation time (daytime, for solar producing households). In some countries it's even illegal to feed energy back into the grid unless you happen to be an energy company.

The ability to store energy and thereby disconnect time of production and use, however, changes all of this. Whether through factory-fresh lithium-ion batteries, swaths of recycled rechargeable nickel-cadmium batteries, or even on-grid liquid metal batteries (being developed by a team around MIT Professor Donald Sadoway), the time will come when households utilize their own energy storage capacity and reduce dependence on energy companies.

In the same way that USB 'chargesticks' today give your smartphone an additional supply of energy when required, cars might just give our homes an additional boost of energy – our appliances and vehicles will share electricity between one another wirelessly, communicating and feeding energy to the unit that requires it most. So while your car or light commercial vehicle can currently only charge your smartphone, computer, power tools and wheelchair, it will someday – at a pinch – also charge your blender, dishwasher and PlayStation.

With cost-efficient energy storage, further new business models will abound. Elon Musk has also supported his cousin Lyndon Rive's start-up SolarCity, an energy provider and solar installation company built on a rental/usage model that's consistent with Zero Ownership.

Recycling through domestic installation of automotive, industrial and household batteries and solar panels will become commonplace, and home batteries will be controlled by equipment that levels the load between 'in-house' generation and mass-generated energy. We'll surely see community energy-pooling models take off (taking entire towns and villages 'off-grid' through locally generated and stored energy).

With storage a given, the potential for wirelessly transferring energy is immense. Companies such as Convenient Power, Plugless Power, WiTricity, Energous and Power by Proxi will see phenomenal growth while attracting equally significant investment. Market research firm IHS predicts that almost one hundred million devices supporting wireless charging could be on the market by 2015. IKEA's newest line of home furniture allows for wireless charging; Starbucks has rolled out wireless charging in its outlets, and Intel has committed to a completely wireless laptop by 2016, but the applications extend well beyond this to household appliances and lights.

Pike Research projects that wireless power product proliferation will see a three-fold increase in market size by 2022, to $15 billion (*Forbes*, July 24, 2014). As swiftly as USB ports became the standard for charging devices in coffee shops, cars, offices, airplanes and homes, we'll see a rollout of wireless charging across the world. Leading the charge (if you'll again excuse the pun) on the consumer-electronics side is Samsung, which has already implemented it in its Galaxy mobile phones, and Apple, whose Watch uses a simple form of wireless charging. Confident that wireless charging isn't just for consumer electronics, the UK government in August 2015 committed £500 million to road-test highway infrastructure that permits mobile inductive charging.

Europe's traditional energy utility companies have together lost an eye-watering €500 billion in market value over a five-year period through 2014. They are not standing idly by, however, as self-generation and off-grid self-sufficiency takes hold. The clever ones are recognizing that charging – wired or otherwise – is a potentially bountiful opportunity and are taking appropriate measures. As reported in September 2014, Sempra Energy in San Diego plans to install 5,000 electric vehicle charging stations at hundreds of office parks, apartment buildings and condo complexes at a cost of $100 million. The ship hasn't sailed, in other words, and if energy companies can assemble and shift course, they can join a long list of organizations tapping into a revenue stream that previously went to the oil industry.

Cities and Public Infrastructure, Reinvented

In February 2014 the UK's Independent Transport Commission rightly asked the question: "Will autonomous cars be 'cars'?" It was a deceptively simplistic question effectively confirming that we are not talking about an automotive revolution but a mobility revolution.

In order to revolutionize the entire transport system, city infrastructure has to be improved and developed accordingly. Future strategies cannot be divided (as they have been) into public transport, personal transport, air transport, train transport and road travel. They must account for and integrate every aspect of travel, the way a multi-modal consumer does. Building a hub airport on an island or a farmer's field outside of town will become as thoughtless an exercise as building a street to nowhere. It's quite simply a question of 'customer-centricity', realized at an advanced stage.

The impact on public infrastructure goes beyond building highway infrastructure and transport networks, however.

Fully one-third of vehicles driving in central Berlin (and most Western cities, for that matter) are seeking a space in which to park. Fifty-nine percent of the ground area of Los Angeles is devoted to streets and parking; in Chicago it's around forty percent, which is in line with a 'quota' that urban planners have traditionally worked with. Real-estate developers have similarly allocated one parking spot for every two people in an office development in the past (and more if there's no credible public transport system).

At the New Urbanism Annual Congress in Buffalo (June 2014), Chris McCahill, Senior Associate at the State Smart Transportation Initiative (based at the University of Wisconsin-Madison) explained that in Hartford, Connecticut, there was close to one parking spot for every 1,000 square-feet of building area – an almost absurd proportion. In some cities the *requirement* is even greater, at three to four parking spots per 1,000 square-feet of building area (although this is almost never adhered to). The opportunity cost to a city like Hartford (due to loss of productive space and tax revenue) would be over $1,200 per space.

In combination with (dis-)incentives such as congestion charging zones and, in the near future, autonomous vehicles, car-sharing will continue to expand, eliminating private vehicles from in-front of, behind, or under residential buildings. As a consequence we'll see parking lots and streets reclaimed for pedestrian use and parks. There are already high-profile examples of this. In Manhattan a swath of Broadway has been closed for vehicles, instead permitting pedestrians and cyclists to more fully enjoy Times Square. Regent Street in London is also closed for vehicle traffic nearly every weekend during summer.

London's Deputy Mayor for Transport, Isabel Dedring, told me:

"Over the last ten to fifteen years – as a result of a series of interventions like bus lanes, pedestrian safety schemes, urban realm improvements – we've taken roughly a third of the capacity for private vehicles out of central London's road-network. This has been made possible in large part through extensive investment in public transport and associated measures such as car-sharing. There is continuing pressure to create a liveable city centre, and this is extending to cutting vehicle emissions and greening fleets across the city – ours, as well as in the private sector."

The trend is not restricted to the largest cities, either. Reporting from the Urban Land Institute's 2013 conference, Leslie Braunstein explained: "Copenhagen has incrementally transformed a downtown, once dominated by cars and surface parking lots, to one that prioritizes pedestrians and bicyclists. Copenhagen's multi-modal transportation system comprises thirty-six percent bikes, thirty-three percent transit, twenty-three percent cars and seven percent pedestrians. More than half of the city's residents cycle to work or school every day; sixty-three percent say they do so because it's fast, easy and convenient, even in the Scandinavian winter."

It seems then that urban policies that repurpose streets, parking areas and city-centre filling stations do rather well. It's a real opportunity for urban architects and a boon to tired city coffers. At the same time, driverless pods of the future will need (non-central) wireless charging and servicing stations.

A new project in the UK will see around one hundred driverless pods roaming Milton Keynes, in Buckinghamshire, from 2015. With enough room to seat two individuals and their luggage, these pods will be entirely autonomous, controlled by smartphone apps that anyone can use to request a lift. Typical cruising speed will be approximately twelve mph, thanks to electric motors, and each ride is touted to cost £2 (c. €2.50/$3) – around the same as a trip by classic public transportation modes.

Is it a shared car? Is it a bus? Is it a taxi? What will we call it? As these low-speed driverless pods will soon be riding alongside pavements and bicycle paths in Milton Keynes, it seems that the third mode of transportation (that I mentioned in Chapter One) may simply be 'the Pod'.

So what becomes of public transportation? Just as schools won't need so many buses (parents will come to trust driverless pods to do the school run for them), the combination of self-driving technology, shared vehicle business models and tighter urban communities (with repurposed public spaces) means that traditional and underground public transport expansion should come to a halt over the next twenty to thirty years despite rampant urbanization. Instead, the funds will need to be allocated to directional and charging technologies.

The Cato Institute's September 2014 report summarized: "When shared use of autonomous vehicles becomes popular, many people who take transit today will find that car-sharing makes more sense." It also issued a warning: "Although self-driving cars may dominate the roads in twenty years, not a single long-range regional transportation plan has considered the effects of such vehicles."

To me it's clear that London's announcement (October 2014) of £16 billion of investment in (predominantly driverless) underground trains will be the last hardware announcement of this scale for some time, just as Manhattan's new Second Avenue Subway will surely be the last new line to be built in the Big Apple. I expect we'll see a shift toward repurposing of roads and railway tracks alongside a significant shift toward managing the software of the network. Demand and investment will move toward interlinking public and private infrastructure, above ground and subterranean transport systems, and also toward making tracking and V2V technology ubiquitous.

Both Ericsson and Cisco have publicly estimated that by 2020 more than fifty billion devices will be connected via the 'Internet of Things' (IoT, also known as the Internet of Objects and the Internet of Everything; Cisco CEO John Chambers estimates this to be a $19 trillion market). In their book *Resource Revolution*, McKinsey's Stefan Heck and Matt Rogers note that over eighty percent of these devices will be communicating not with an end-user but with *each other*, "working behind the scenes on our behalf." With respect to our mobility, this means we'll have a more seamless user experience. It also means there is enormous financial potential – with a lot of buses and trains to retrofit.

Here's a scenario: Going from home to a business meeting in another city, today's toddler (I'll call him George) will in tomorrow's world use a driverless pod that picks him up at home and connects to a chain of pods in the subway tunnel. After ten minutes of smooth motion, George will transfer to a high-speed rail service that knows he's on his way; his automatically reserved seat will blink for identification as he walks by. As he sits down, his meeting partner and family will be able to track George's whereabouts and know he's on-time. The service will take him to Urbania, where he might jump onto a motorized, self-navigating bicycle for the last mile of travel. On his way home George's travel app has already hailed a shared-use UberGoogleLyft-mobile, which takes him to a different station with the quickest train link to his favourite restaurant. He will have been charged for the entire trip on a per-mile or per-minute basis and overall it will compare to what he spent previously for owning and fuelling a car. George cannot even conceive of owning his own vehicle (either as a company car or privately) the way his grandfather did. Instead, he revels in several extra days per year in productivity – time previously spent sitting in traffic.

Construction and Infrastructure: The Aftermath

"The so-called McMansion will become the new multi-family home for the poor." (CNN, June 16, 2008)

As urbanization continues apace, automated home delivery flourishes, wireless charging lanes are installed in parking lots and express-lanes, city centres are reimagined and parking spaces are repurposed, suburbia will experience considerable turmoil. Shopping malls and 'strip malls' will die a slow (and to my mind, a welcome) death. What will happen to the ugly box-stores of generations past? Might there be potential in recycling the building materials used at Sears, J.C. Penney and Wal-Mart? Or can those stores be simply be repurposed into thousands of multi-local 3D printing sites for batteries and autonomous vehicle pods? Perhaps Wal-Mart should be talking with Local Motors!

As the nature and scope of infrastructure work changes, so too will construction companies need to adjust. Zero Emissions will not just apply to vehicles, but also to buildings; there is a clear trend toward zero-carbon housing (or even negative-emission constructions – buildings that produce more energy and clean air than they consume). Homes, apartment buildings and offices will consistently require charging stations (wired or wireless). Just as 3D printing will produce vehicles, disrupting the value chain, it will also be used to create building components, transforming logistics in the construction industry. But I digress. Suffice it to say, a reliance on public works and highway building projects, allocated wherever the flow of traffic is high and obeying the ancient 'predict and provide' philosophy of transport planning, will abruptly end.

Anyone still worried about data privacy and the transparency of our mobility has missed the boat. All our movements are already tracked via our mobile phones, which through the use of big data proves as beneficial to end users and city planners as it is disappointing for construction companies.

I've previously mentioned INRIX – a company measuring the productivity impact of traffic congestion. Little known is that it has a technology that anonymously and silently crowd-sources traffic data from *185 million* mobile phones, connected cars, trucks and delivery vehicles worldwide, with the lofty aim of solving traffic worldwide. Beyond merely measuring and discussing congestion, INRIX also aims to reduce road congestion with the data it has at its disposal. By actively and continually shifting the recommendations of millions of GPS satellite navigation systems (including on smartphones), its software will effectively steer the flow of traffic to make better use of existing infrastructure. Similarly, Google's Waze has become a must-have navigation and social networking application for over 50 million users worldwide – providing real-time traffic data unmatched by reactive systems of the past. As urbanization continues, distances travelled shorten and highways are used more efficiently, construction companies will need to pave something other than roads and parking lots.

Installing wireless charging lanes for use by public transport vehicles, taxis (those that remain, that is) and personal transit pods will become a key public-private partnership initiative in cities. Chun-Taek Rim, Professor of Nuclear and Quantum Engineering at Korea's Advanced Institute of Science & Technology wrote in an editorial to the *Korea Herald*:

> "The times call for a smart road system that incorporates IT to enable driverless driving, wireless charging and safer driving. The biggest advantage of smart roads is that since they do not require land compensation, the construction budget is greatly reduced."

Construction firms with a history of delivering toll-road projects might have an advantage. One entrepreneur in the UK successfully built, operated and charged for use of a private toll road between Bath and Bristol for six months when the main road was logged with roadworks. Similar projects will emerge for wireless charging lanes, perhaps during large sporting or entertainment events.

Logistics gets Logical

In 2006 the US trucking industry employed 3.4 million drivers; each had to undertake a demanding confirmation procedure before getting hired. What happens to these drivers when the transition toward self-driving vehicles takes place? True, even if trucks become autonomous – as Mercedes-Benz and Volvo have planned for 2025 at the latest – there remains the need for someone in an operator's seat (somewhere) to monitor the operations of the system and the delivery process. The job description will change from driver to software operator.

Safety and congestion should improve when autonomous technology propagates. In order to monitor the truck, however, operators may still require rest breaks, especially as the responsibility of operating a fleet of multi-trailer vehicles at the same time brings with it greater potential for stress. Much like air-traffic controllers, freight forwarders will be even more bound by a duty of care toward their operators.

As trust in the self-driving ability of the machines grows, freight trucks will be driven in shifts around the clock, improving productivity (and lowering costs). Current commercial vehicle driving restrictions (in Europe) will be lifted, as electric trucks won't emit the noise and carbon dioxide and particulates they did. The frequency of deliveries will increase significantly, but what does this mean for warehouse capacity? Could it be reduced, as more deliveries can be undertaken on a single journey? Many factories (including the most efficient automobile facilities) already operate on a just-in-time supply basis – we can expect this to expand up, down and across the value chain. In many industries self-driving vehicles (and delivery drones) will force the entire supply chain and logistics network to be re-designed.

Financial Services for the Three Zeroes Economy

In 2013 Chunka Mui, the distinguished innovation analyst, asked in a *Forbes Magazine* article: "Will auto insurers survive their collision with driverless cars?" The answer is similar to the automobile industry: not without ground-up, carte blanche reinvention.

In the US the market for auto insurance is worth $200 billion annually, with premiums calculated on the basis of accident rates and vehicle usage. However, the current model for automotive insurance is doomed in a future with dwindling accidents and a significant change in the usage model. Already the market is a barely-profitable model (operationally speaking) in most Western markets – claims and administration costs together amount to around ninety-six or ninety-seven percent of each dollar, euro or pound taken in as a premium, leaving an operating margin (without investment returns) of only a few percentage points. With thousands of large and small players vying for market share, competition in this sleepy industry is intense and all-consuming. The industry is only lucrative as car insurance is the sole (or one of very few) mandatory insurance, meaning that firms use it as a point of entry (and a basis for cross-selling) to the widest possible cross-section of customers. Zero Accidents and Zero Ownership removes *both* claims and premiums. What's left (but not for long) is the administrative cost.

I've spent more than twelve years both running and consulting insurance teams, so I am still reasonably confident that the industry will survive, albeit on a smaller scale and with a raft of new and innovative players that will rock the boat of incumbents. Already companies like Fairzekering in Holland, DirectLine and Autosaint in the UK, Metromile in California and even the giants Allstate, Aviva and Allianz offer telematics-supported usage-based car insurance policies. In the same vein ZipCar users are offered shared-vehicle insurance policies and Uber operators will be offered (or required) to have driver and passenger insurance in place. Looking ahead, anyone using personal transport pods may opt to insure themselves through a form of travel or operator insurance – the list of potential products is as endless as the creativity of the underwriters and sales force. It just requires a bit of pressure and creativity (when the business environment gives you lemons, make lemonade).

But what about the rest of the financial services industry? Can it adapt? Well, clearly the automotive leasing and financing industries are impelled to change. In theory fewer accidents mean fewer replacement vehicles and lower ownership means a reduced need to finance vehicles. But I won't paint a doomsday scenario here – quite the opposite. The opportunities for financial services are substantial.

Erich Ebner von Eschenbach, CEO at BMW Financial Services noted for a 2012 KPMG report on the status of the automotive leasing and financing industry: "The fundamental change in customer behaviour requires new, flexible products and services that address the trend from car ownership to car usage." Another executive vice president at a Japanese automotive financial services company noted: "We closely monitor possible shifts in the automotive industry with regard to electric vehicles and their implications on our financial services. Battery management could be incorporated into leasing services if it becomes a key element of managing electric vehicles, for instance." In fact, when consumers buy a Renault ZOE or Twizy electric vehicle today they are required to lease the battery. This effectively continues a shift in the value chain of automotive toward the (financial) services organizations, which once started with *optional* leasing and financing.

In July 2014 London's transport system changed to allow contactless payments on any route via debit or credit card; New York and Washington DC are expected to follow suit by 2019. Similarly, most bicycle or car-sharing models rely entirely on account-linked cards for identification and payment. At the very least, financing the transaction creates benefits for Visa, Mastercard and American Express – done right, providing pathways for the network will aid the seamlessness of mobility provision. With regard to a more holistic mobility approach, the KPMG study also stated: "Customers will require access to multi-mode transportation (bus, train, car, bike and plane) while only paying a flat-rate for the whole package. Such mobility concepts will increase the need… to align even more closely with other mobility providers."

Clever financial services companies will also find themselves setting up the billing model for the aforementioned wireless charging lanes.

Last but certainly not least is that new business models, construction and infrastructure projects and start-up companies require funding, investment and advising. New companies that emerge will look to debt and equity markets for capital. The financial industry will continue to provide the grease that keeps the wheels of the mobility revolution in motion.

Three Zeroes Take to the Sky

The innovation and pursuit of electric autonomous vehicles is not limited to land.

We've become somewhat familiar with unmanned, electric drones flying above our heads – as toys in shopping centres and city parks, and as prototypes for Amazon deliveries. Taking the idea a little larger, Airbus has developed prototypes and began building the production plant for fully electric two- and four-seat aircraft with lithium-ion polymer batteries, which it demonstrated to the press at the 2014 Farnborough International Airshow. Adding another 'zero' to their brainstorming, Airbus has also conceived a model that relocates the cockpit of commercial airliners to another part of the plane altogether. In 2014 the company was issued a patent for a windowless cockpit, located under the nose cone of the aircraft. The rationale is simple: today's cockpit not only takes up considerable space that could be used to seat passengers and increase revenue, but also dictates a certain nose-cone shape and requires windows on the front of the plane that together reduce fuel efficiency. As part of the patent Airbus is investigating moving the entire cockpit to an area that's otherwise unused and has no revenue-generating potential. Huge wraparound screens in the cockpit would give the illusion of windows and, for all intents and purposes, it would be like sitting in a conventional plane. The screens would stream real-time footage of the view in front of the plane using cameras, enhancing the pilot's vision by giving him or her the capability to zoom in or out on approaching terrain.

As one enthusiast wrote on the airliners.net blog: "If you think about it, it's quite practical with today's technology. When you're flying in IFR conditions and performing a Cat III approach, you might as well forget that you have windows. With synthetic-vision systems already being used, they just need to become more dependable with redundancy built in." Another noted: "It will happen eventually, and even old timers will adopt it, because the rendered image will be ultra HD 3D etc. Of course I'm not sure on-board pilots will still exist by then."

Taking it yet one step further, and given the advent of the sharing-economy even for private air-travel (mentioned earlier in the book), it's fair to say that the three zeroes have taken to the sky.

Any manufacturer intent on being (or remaining) part of the future of mobility should examine examples of other industries in transformation and look toward technologies implemented in aviation and the computer industry. Countless examples of industry leaders who have failed should serve as clear warning shots across the bow of traditional car manufacturers. Who then will be the winners and losers after this wave of transformation in the automobile industry? Quite clearly, those mass-market manufacturers that haven't recognized the trend will lose, becoming road-kill. Just like Smith Corona, Kodak, Atari and Commodore.

The combined impacts of the three zeroes featured in this book will have a staggering effect that cannot be ignored or postponed. The list of further affected industries is lengthy. I have given a few examples directly associated with cars (and one that isn't), but the impact is much wider. Next time you are discussing the impact of urbanization and *The Three Zeroes* at the dinner table (and I hope that you do), consider the associated fate and future opportunities of:

- First and second tier suppliers to the automobile industry
- First and second tier suppliers to oil and energy companies
- Auto dealers, distributors and repair shops
- Electrical appliance manufacturers and dealers
- Highway-diner cooks and service staff
- Energy-transmission line repairmen
- Fuel tank cleaners and refurbishers
- Scrap-metal traders and recyclers
- Tollbooth collectors
- Filling station purveyors
- Home improvement shops
- Golf-cart developers
- Pavers and line painters
- Keymakers and locksmiths
- Elevator and escalator companies
- Industrial and electrical wire producers
- Suburban swimming pool installers and cleaners
- The Avon and Tupperware salesperson
- Greenpeace and the Worldwide Fund for Nature.

Conclusion

So, am I off my rocker? Mad to suggest that the world will be a vastly different place in the not-so-distant future? Is the Mobility Revolution really coming? Will we really be hanging up our keys for good? Will this change the way I live? To all of these I say, 'perhaps'.

I think change will happen in our lifetime and much sooner than we expect. The next vehicle you buy may just be your last. It will most likely be at least an electric hybrid, almost certainly with a connection to a grid, and will include autonomous driving features. Make sure there are pictures of you driving it – your grandchildren won't believe you.

Naturally my view and proposed timescale is clearly influenced by living in two of the world's great and most advanced transportation centres, far removed from the rural landscape where I grew up and hundreds of miles from the nearest subway amidst cows and the ubiquitous pickup truck.

Since I started researching and writing this book around 2012 and even since the first printing in 2014, there have been countless announcements and many more projected entrants in the areas of Zero Emissions, Zero Accidents and Zero Ownership, including Apple. In business and in society, a lot more people are coming round to this way of thinking and I've been fortunate to receive progressively more positive feedback on my message. The blogosphere, Twittersphere, LinkedIn and popular media have been awash with articles detailing the impending revolution, but from experts to consultants and journalists, nobody knows the future for certain. We're just here to help guide the strategic thinking process.

Good luck and enjoy the ride.

Thank you

Writing a book is an undertaking that requires many partners; I'd like to thank a few who have contributed to making this project come to life.

First, thank you to the people I've consulted and interviewed – formally and informally – whose thoughts went into this book: the visionary Ola Källenius and knowledgeable Wilfried Steffen at Daimler, the inspiring Hugo Spowers and Nick Keppel-Palmer at Riversimple, Cristiano Carlutti and Maurits Aalberse at Qoros, Allan Pedersen at Polarax Capital, Ulrich Quay at BMW iVentures, Mike Shier at Streetventory, Alex Schoch – formerly at Tesla, Christine Thompson and Robert Lavia – formerly of Veremonte and Formula E, Christophe Arnaud at Bolloré and Blue Point London, Chelsea Sexton at Plug-In America, Paul Stith at EV Grid and Project Green Onramp, Matt Stevens at CrossChasm, David Pillinger – formerly at ZipCar Europe, Chris McCahill at the State Smart Transportation Initiative, Florian Rothfuss at the Fraunhofer Institute, Catherine Kargas at Marcon, the team at Mojomotors, Charles Jennings at 70:20:10, Margy Wiklinska at ZF Friedrichshafen, as well as Jeremy Deering and Jeremy North – of Torotrack and Dearman Engine Company, respectively.

Isabel Dedring and Nicholas Short have each been very generous in giving their insights into the political motivation to drive forward the Three Zeroes in the fascinating city of London. And a big thank you, also, to a number of unnamed sources at BMW, Volkswagen, Jaguar Land Rover and Allianz, as well as my clients and interview partners through the course of writing this book.

I'm grateful to Wanda Wallace and Edison Hudson, who each provided a spark of inspiration for me to write this book. Chris Emerson at Airbus and Joachim Taiber at Clemson University's International Center for Automotive Research have each been the source of many ideas, and even more contacts. Similarly, Amy Birchall and Jacqueline Lim at Volans have connected me well and have been fun sparring partners, as have Ezra Goldman, founder of Upshift in San Francisco, and Markus Merz at Monocom.

Thank you as well to early readers of the book, especially Markku Wilenius at the Finland Futures Research Center and Andrew Howe, to Jeremy Thompson who chose to publish this book and to Richard Lane – an excellent editor, as passionate about the subject matter as he is about correcting the written word. A very special thank you to Nils Poschwatta for taking his exceptional talents and time away from designing future cars in order to conceive this book's cover.

Michael Mandat and Gottfried Zach at Progenium, Thomas Pütter and Tony Benitez at Ancora, and Simon Court at Value-Partnership are excellent colleagues and progressive-thinking consulting partners, who have each contributed to this book in their own way.

Most importantly, I thank my wife and family for patience and unwavering support. It is for my two sons that I have written this book – your lives and careers will benefit most from The Mobility Revolution.

About the Author and Editor

Lukas Neckermann is a strategy advisor, entrepreneur and speaker with twenty years of leadership experience in automotive, media and financial services in the US, the UK and Germany. His passion is for guiding corporate visions toward strategy and implementation through innovation processes, planning and staff engagement.

After beginning his career at radio station WVBR in Ithaca, New York, Lukas joined BMW Group in Munich, where he was responsible for interactive media and Internet marketing as well as licensing BMWs for video games including from Sony and Electronic Arts. At BMW, he also developed the communication strategy for the Z8 and worked in Internal Marketing Consulting. After BMW, he held significant leadership roles at financial services company Allianz, including Head of Business Development for Allianz Automotive. He left the Allianz Group after several years as Commercial Director and member of the Executive Board at Euler Hermes in the UK and Ireland.

Independently, Lukas was a member of the core team of the first Open Source Car project (TheOSCarproject.org), co-founded Monoventure Srl (a real-estate investment company in Romania), MN Innovative Communication Inc. in New York, Neckermann Ltd in London and the Freckleray brand. He works as an associate with several leading management consulting companies, is a Fellow of the Institute of Leadership and Management (ILM) and is Senior Advisor to two start-up companies in electric, autonomous and shared mobility.

Lukas is an Adjunct Instructor at New York University, has lectured and taught courses to thousands of executives from over forty countries and has spoken at countless conferences on marketing, business development, communication, leadership and corporate education. He holds a Bachelor's degree in Science and Technology Studies from Cornell University and an MBA from New York University's Stern School of Business. He divides his time between London, Munich and Upstate New York.

Richard Lane is an automotive journalist specializing in low-carbon transportation and sustainable design. Despite a deep interest in urban mobility initiatives, it's the cars themselves – oafish, outmoded cars – that most vigorously stoke his passion for mobility. Richard is on the editorial roster at *evo magazine*, following positions at Green Car Design and as deputy editor of ecomento.com. He has had the privilege of road-testing machines including the Tesla Roadster and BMW i8.

Notes